the student. I learned to an extent I didn't imagine prior. I have started to put into action small steps toward sustainability. I have the author to thank for that education. The author's dedication toward educating the reader is outstanding.

**Timothy Lange**, Teacher, coach, administrator, superintendent secondary education for 33 years

What people are saying about

# Finding Sustainability

In the USA 30+ million small businesses employ 47+% of the private workforce. This means, there is no sustainable future without small business. That is to say, future generations will not enjoy a stable climate, a viable biosphere, an equitable and opportunity rich economy, global peace, justice and inclusion, without small business making all of those things part of their core mission and business.

So what does it take to turn a small business into a sustainability leadership lighthouse? For one thing, it's not the same journey as a global corporation or a forward-thinking government organization. Small business is edgier. There's less room for error, less buffer in the face of external threats. Small business has a more intimate interdependence with its employees, local community, suppliers, customers. Small business takes a lot of heart. It's more personal.

In this book, you hear the rare and important voice of a small business owner taken by surprise as the world around him starts signaling that his company's core product is out of sync with a sustainable future. We are talking about the iconic plastic bag.

This is an important book because it tells a very personal story with enormous honesty and humility. Why didn't this business owner do what most small business owners choose to do and just tune out these signals in order to get through another quarter? How could he take on the unimaginable risks of pivoting his entire business, when so much was at stake, the market wasn't demanding it yet and the risks and challenges of pivoting ahead of the market were so enormous? And what did his co-owner, employees and family make of all this?

This is the anatomy of 21st century leadership. It is personal, vulnerable, honest and it happens in the humble arena of one day at a time. I'm so glad Trent has written this for us and about us.

**Leith Sharp**, Director & Lead Faculty Executive Education for Sustainability Leadership Harvard T.H. Chan School of Public Health

*Finding Sustainability* offers a compass for family-owned businesses to navigate uncertain waters that threaten the very backbone of the company. The quest for in-depth understanding of environmental sustainability provides a compelling road map to uncovering creative solutions that are not obvious. I highly recommend *Finding Sustainability* to businesses of any size who are searching how to navigate a purpose-driven transformation rooted in sustainability, faith and the quest for meaning.

**Patrick Lindner**, Senior Executive for Fortune 500 and family-owned corporations

*Finding Sustainability* takes the reader on a true journey. As the author journeys through nature with his family, he realizes that he must also embark on a sustainability journey with his organization. Throughout his journey, his faith and commitment to his family, his company, his employees and his community lead him to learn what sustainability means and how to embrace it in order to ensure the long-term viability of his company. But sustainability in a family-owned, petroleum-based, packaging company presents real challenges. The reader learns about these challenges along with steps for overcoming them that can be applied to any organization. Ultimately, *Finding Sustainability* provides the motivation and rationale for bringing sustainability into our personal and professional lives.

**Linda Krzykowski**, Associate Vice Provost, University at Albany

I spent 33 years as an educator and coach, working hard to help develop young minds. In reading *Finding Sustainability*, I became

# Finding Sustainability

The Personal and Professional Journey
of a Plastic Bag Manufacturer

# Finding Sustainability

## The Personal and Professional Journey of a Plastic Bag Manufacturer

Trent A. Romer

BUSINESS
BOOKS

Winchester, UK
Washington, USA

## JOHN HUNT PUBLISHING

First published by Business Books, 2021
Business Books is an imprint of John Hunt Publishing Ltd., No. 3 East St., Alresford,
Hampshire SO24 9EE, UK
office@jhpbooks.com
www.johnhuntpublishing.com
www.johnhuntpublishing.com/business-books

For distributor details and how to order please visit the 'Ordering' section on our website.

Text copyright: Trent A. Romer 2020

ISBN: 978 1 78904 601 4
978 1 78904 602 1 (ebook)
Library of Congress Control Number: 2020933105

A CIP catalogue record for this book is available from the British Library.

Design: Stuart Davies

Printed and bound by CPI Group (UK) Ltd, Croydon, CR0 4YY

We operate a distinctive and ethical publishing philosophy in
all areas of our business, from our global network of authors to
production and worldwide distribution.

# Contents

To my mother
The writer in me is rooted in you

## Introduction

# Journey Toward Sustainability

### The Present

We climbed into the van at 3:00 a.m. We were the last pickup.

The fourteen-seat van had just two seats left open, unfortunately not together. We were packed in like sardines, and the back windows were cracked but couldn't be rolled down. The expanse of the ocean below was illuminated only by the light of the moon, where the shoreline appeared as dark objects with dim shadows. We snaked rapidly up steep, curving roads, back and forth, back and forth, for miles with no guard rails. I began to sweat, and my stomach turned. I kept reminding myself this would all be worth it. I wondered how my new wife was making out a few rows up.

We were racing to the summit of Mount Haleakala in Haleakala National Park, Maui, Hawaii. It was a clear and cold early morning, and when the sun rose at 6:30, we would be watching from 10,000 feet above sea level.

We arrived at 5:30 to find the stars seemingly within arm's reach. The temperature rose slowly, and our chatter faded as though talking would reduce the visibility. The dark suppressed the light for as long as it could, then the night sky gave way to stratified layers of blue, which grew increasingly lighter toward the distant line of the ocean. Blues transitioned to oranges and yellows, and the intensity of light narrowed to a specific spot on the horizon. When the sun broke through, rays of light pierced the sky in all directions, shooting through the oranges and blues above and striking our faces. The brilliant dot grew larger.

The new day began.

Our tour had provided bikes for us to ride back down the mountain, and the descent offered spectacular panoramic views of the ocean reflecting the sun's light. The same roads that had given me nausea on the way up now gave me an overwhelming sense of liberation, freedom and appreciation of nature's beauty as we coasted down.

Newlyweds on our honeymoon, my wife and I shared that sunrise moment—a powerful feeling engrained in my memory, the feeling that began our married life.

This is the feeling I chase.

\* \* \*

What if the foundation of your family business were threatened by something out of your control? What if the livelihood of seventy employees and their families were at stake, as the license to operate your business became called into question? What if fifty-seven years of family history, grown through generations of hard work and sacrifice, were at risk?

What if the reason were actually one with which you fundamentally agreed?

I am the third-generation co-owner of a family-owned and -operated plastic bag manufacturing company. Ocean plastics and the anti-plastic environmental narrative surrounding our industry has had a profound effect on our business and on me personally.

In May 2018, I began my journey to learn how our business could navigate the new challenges that threaten our very existence. Over the eighteen months that followed, I traveled to Amsterdam to visit a plastic-free supermarket and attended a European Plastics Strategy conference for manufacturers and converters in Brussels. I applied to, was accepted by and attended a week-long Executive Education on Sustainability at Harvard University in Cambridge, Massachusetts. I went to Chicago to exhibit at a four-day packaging trade show, to Seattle to participate in the week-long Sustainable Packaging Coalition

Conference and on a plant tour of a material-recycling facility in Albany, New York. I also visited Yosemite National Park in the Sierra Nevada Mountains.

These experiences—combined with speaking with countless people, reading reports, books and articles, watching videos, following sustainability social media sources and listening to podcasts—helped me form a new company vision. An unintended result of all this was a new sense of fulfillment in better aligning my faith with our business.

Embracing a sustainable mindset has allowed me to view sustainability as a place where business meets faith.

After twenty-seven years in the plastics business and a year and a half immersed in sustainability, I've decided it is time to document my journey. What seemed a potential death blow to our company has become an opportunity to take part in a new packaging economy. I want to share my personal and professional story.

This is not an exhaustive education on sustainable packaging, nor does it propose any absolute conclusions for the future state of plastics. My story is told from my perspective of working all my life in this family business, of always striving to be better, regardless of circumstances, and of my experiences growing up as a person with deep roots in faith.

My hope is that my story will have broad appeal to those looking for a path to reducing ocean plastics and becoming part of a new plastics circular economy. More narrowly, my story is written to appeal to those seeking a sense of opportunity in creating more sustainable companies based upon circular principals and to inspire a call to action for the years to come. The narrowest and most direct goal for my book is to help those who might feel similarly pressured in facing seemingly insurmountable challenges in today's environmental crises. This is especially relevant for those who feel largely responsible for the legacy of businesses woven through their personal and family lives.

What follows is my journey toward sustainability, powered by education, experiences, interactions and images, all of which have served as motivation, information and directional guides. These elements of my journey are now embedded in my mind and have had a transformational impact on how I think, both personally and as a business-owner. They combine to frame the extent of the issue of plastics in our environment, a means to deal with this issue and a renewed clarity of purpose through sustainability.

# Part I

# Education

# Chapter 1

# Too Large To Ignore

## Family Business History and the Challenge Ahead

My deep connection to the environment grows, in part, from my childhood memories of our family summer vacations. We camped on the islands of Lake George in upstate New York, a freshwater lake extending thirty-two miles north-to-south and varying between one and three miles across; over 170 islands dot the length of the lake, with camping allowed on about fifty of them.

After we arrived at the marina, it would take two or three trips to transport our gear from shore to our chosen campsite. The island we typically called home was isolated and small, with just a few campsites, and felt like our own personal property to explore and conquer.

Of course, nature's fury always quelled any idea of conquering. The week typically saw thunderstorms, which gave us some anxiety, as our tent blew side-to-side and rain poured down. We'd ride out the storm by digging trenches around the base of the tent and securing all things outside to the ground.

However, bright sunshine always followed. Days of swimming, fishing, water skiing and boating gave way to nights of playing cards, storytelling and campfires. On July nights, the sun in upstate New York sets around 8:30 p.m. The surface of the water became calm at nightfall as our activities on the lake ended. Dimming daylight was replaced by campfire, and the only sounds were the crackle of burning wood, the small waves of the lake lapping the shore, a few crickets and distant motorboats speeding home before the lake became blanketed by darkness. Eventually, faraway campfires across the water were the only markings of the other islands.

The peace and isolation gave us something that I already had in abundance but was in short supply for my parents: time. Time to look, to listen, to absorb our surroundings and to enjoy each other's company.

* * *

In May of 2018, I found myself at a crossroads. Our 57-year-old family business manufacturing plastic bags faced growing anti-plastic public sentiment, which threatened the survival of our company and my ability to support both my immediate family and all the families our business employs. To exacerbate the situation, my heart and my head agreed with the sentiment. I felt compelled to act to preserve our environment and, by extension, my children's future.

Our family business dates back to 1961. In the 1950s, my maternal grandfather Donald Strevell was a traveling salesman for the Simonds Saw and Steel Company, selling high-quality saws in the Northeast. In the days of pay phones and few major highways, when a daytrip of today took him three days, he often traveled for weeks at a time.

To make ends meet, my grandmother Fulvia signed on as a salesperson for a greeting card company, and my mother recalls sitting in the car as my grandmother went door to door in wealthy suburban neighborhoods, looking for clients.

Eventually, my grandfather's travel away from the family pushed him and my grandmother to start a family business. They began to sell decorative packaging out of the barn behind their house. My grandfather was the primary salesperson, while my grandmother, uncle and mother processed orders, prepared shipments and helped handle the paperwork. Their 1962 business card spoke to their charisma and dedication to their early customers:

Operation Thoughtfulness
When it is so easy to be nice and nice to be liked, who can afford not to be both?
The Box and Bow
Fulvia and Don Strevell

I still have the Box and Bow business card at my desk, where I work each day.

After my parents were married, my father joined my mother's family's business, and the name was changed to Clear View Bag Company, Inc.

As the tenth of eleven children, my father had never been handed anything. He had worked with his close-knit family to care for one another, patiently waiting his turn and working hard to achieve his dreams. And this is exactly how he ran his business. He is humble, smart and incredibly supportive of the people employed by him. He always led by example rather than words, showing us how to work hard while treating all customers, competitors and employees with respect, regardless of circumstances.

Just like my grandmother, my mother made untold sacrifices to support the family business. She was a nurse before surrendering her career to raise my brother, my sister and me, while supporting and helping my father in the growing business. None of us—not my brother, my sister nor I, not to mention the business—would be what we are today without her sacrifice. The immense gravity of her choice is matched only by our collective gratitude.

I have twenty-eight first cousins on my father's side, so, as the business grew into custom manufacturing of cellophane and polyethylene products, his large family became a major source of labor, loyalty and support. His people instincts and business acumen provided work and steady growth for all employees for more than forty years. He even moved the business several times to accommodate growth, and whenever asked his highest priority for his business, he always responded, "to provide for the families we employ."

In 2007, my father sold the business to my brother and me, and we have owned it ever since.

My brother and sister and I grew up in the house in which the business started, where the barn that originally housed my grandparents' tiny factory served years later as my adolescent weight room. My mother has lived in that house her entire life, and my parents still live there. Going home for holidays every year brings back powerful memories of childhood and of the origins of our family business. The risk my grandparents took is in the air of that house, the growing pains my parents experienced—which we kids never knew—is real, and the rich history of our large family and business is palpable.

As third-generation family business owners, my brother and I know that the odds are stacked against us. Seventy percent of family businesses do not make it to a second generation. Eighty-eight percent fail to make it to a third generation. Ninety-seven percent fail to make it to a fourth generation.[1]

Both my brother and I earned four-year Bachelor's Degrees before joining the family business, and our father was our main source of practical education, particularly in our early years after college. The lessons we learned from him could not be found in any textbook or seminar.

Early in our managerial careers, my father gave us plenty of rope to mold the business for our future. That rope hung us at times, as we stumbled to find our way. To remain competitive required technology upgrades, streamlined processes, set procedures and buy-in from employees. Over time, we altered from a generic bag-maker to a custom bag-maker with short lead-times.

The changes we made created some friction, especially with long-term employees who felt tremendous loyalty to my father. Although in the name of bringing the company to a new level, the effect of our changes on employees and on us could be trying. My father's patience allowed us to attempt different things and, many times, to fail. We learned painful lessons that made us stronger in the long run. Neither of us will ever forget those early years, and we will always be grateful to the people who allowed us to find our way.

Change has been no stranger to us. We have migrated away from generic stock bags and simple constructions to increasingly complex construction, materials and prints. We have also invested heavily in automation, both in the plant, with multi-million dollar equipment, and in our customer interaction software. We know that, if we do not change as things around us change, we will disappear.

We currently employ seventy people and increasingly pursue custom package-manufacturing, from recloseable bags to mailers to high-end prints. We provide packaging for both major, highly-recognizable brands and small, relatively-unknown names. While many of the bags we manufacture are found at supermarkets and big box stores, we generally cater to lower-volume orders, through which we can help those who need custom packaging for specific items and grow with their business needs as the years unfold.

My brother and I try to combine the entrepreneurship and client focus of our grandparents with the employee focus and humility of our parents, all within the modern technology-driven business modes today.

Besides business lessons from my father, I looked outside our business for ideas on how to learn and improve. As a smaller-sized company, we did not have a corporate training program. So, after graduating from Hamilton College, I began pursuing a Master's Degree in Education at the University at Albany, thinking I wanted to be a teacher. However, a few years into the program, I knew I would stay with our family business. I finished my Education MS and enrolled in a Master's in Business Administration, earning my MBA five years later. Nine years of night school netted me two Master's Degrees, and since then I have taken online courses, attended multiple conferences and read a lot in order to keep shaping our company.

In June 2018, the cover of *National Geographic Magazine* brought our company and me personally to our biggest challenge yet.

The cover shows a profile view of the ocean, a third of the cover above the waterline and two-thirds below. Above the water, the image appears to be an iceberg, but below the surface the true image is revealed as a carry-out plastic bag. The white plastic pokes through the surface of the ocean in a pyramid shape like an iceberg, providing a powerful revelation of how we neglectfully interact with and negatively impact our oceans and our planet.

The ocean plastics epidemic began to gain notoriety, most notably with the Blue Planet II television episode on the BBC in 2017. *National Geographic* was one of the first major media outlets to hit the United States more directly.

For many years, the issue of plastic pollution had seemed to me too large to tackle. I was just a small manufacturer with a business to support. What could I possibly do?

However, now it seemed too large to ignore. I did not feel great about the product we made. Our main raw material is plastic, and pushing for ever-increasing sales was a benefit to me, my family and our employee's families, whom our business supports. I knew that plastics help our lives every day in many ways, from food protection to medical devices to car and airplane parts.[2] Still, more sales also meant more plastic in circulation, and I learned that eight million tons of plastic winds up in the ocean each year.[3] The plastics conundrum lies in the great value to our everyday lives and the simultaneous damage to the environment if plastic is treated as disposable rather than as a resource.

I had my own personal conundrum. Up until May 2018,

I had done very little to explore alternatives or even flesh out my feelings. I'd had a hard time acting, until I began to think about my grandparents and parents and their decision-making processes.

I am an academic at heart. I was very fortunate to go to college and graduate school for my formal education. My decision-making is rooted in my educational background. My mother attended post-secondary nursing school, but neither my grandparents nor my father were ever afforded the opportunities of higher education. While naturally intelligent, my grandparents and parents "trusted their guts" to make tough business decisions, based on their experiences. The idea of relying on feeling rather than theory seemed foreign to my thought process, but I began to think that my situation needed intuition to trump my usual structured style.

Years of experience and contemplation led me to indescribable feelings. My gut told me that it was time to change. The *National Geographic* image made me understand that this is real, this is big and it would be transformative in some way directly affecting me, my family, our employees and our business. The article forced me to confront my own thoughts, along with determining what our company was going to do in the wake of the tsunami of anti-plastic narrative.

In my mind, I had an image of the path I had been on for so many years, abruptly ending at the edge of a body of water. To one side lay a path to short-term survival, in continuing to operate in the same way and provide the same plastic products we always had. In the opposite direction lay the way of preservation and doing the right thing for future generations. To choose short-term survival was to potentially sacrifice the planet's future, while to choose preservation would have an impact on our short-term survival. I wanted to both survive and preserve, but taking both paths was impossible.

Now my mind saw a third choice: a boat floated at the shore's edge that could lead—at least initially—to education, in order to clarify the decision I needed to make on shore.

I chose the boat.

I got in with no oars and no direction. My destination was unclear, but I knew where to start finding maps for my journey. I knew I would return eventually to the point of choosing. For now, the unknown was strangely comfortable.

As I left the shore, I glanced back and saw the survival path continuing into the future, similar to the one I had traveled to this point, albeit with a lot more bumps due to deteriorating public views on plastics. The preservation path was barely visible in the short term, while the long-term benefits seemed too distant to think about realistically. Being in a boat in the water was a new adventure.

All my life, I have believed that hard work wins out in the long run. The anti-plastic narrative made me double down on this belief, working extra hard and seeking the right direction for our business and for me personally—before it's too late.

## Chapter 2

# Find Your Maps

## The Circular Economy and New Plastics Economy

In August 2019, four friends and I went on a two-day overnight canoe trip with a guide to the Saint Regis canoe area in the Adirondack Mountains in upstate New York, the only designated canoe area, closed to all motorized vehicles, in New York State. The state land has no private residences or commercialization. Over fifty ponds and small lakes are spread across 18,400 acres, very few of the ponds or lakes accessed without a portage in which everything must be carried. Our trip included seven different portages as we made our way through eight unique bodies of water. Throughout our two days, we saw only a handful of people canoeing, dwarfed by the amount of wildlife.

We set up camp late in the afternoon in as remote a place as I have ever been, our elevated make-shift campsite overlooking a small pond that connected two larger bodies of water. Nothing moved. There was no sound. The silence settled my mind, sharpened my senses and provided new clarity of thought.

The sense of nothingness was broken by the sight and sound of water pushed aside as a loon touched down and skidded to a halt on the bird's watery landing strip. A deer peeked through the vegetation and stared as if we were a museum exhibit. The shadow of a soaring hawk touched the surface of the pond. Nothing was happening, yet everything was occurring.

Packing for the trip had made me begin to fully comprehend the concept of economy. The real estate in my small backpack was devoted to essentials, and luxury items like pillows and towels did not make the cut. In addition to our backpacks, at every portage we carried the canoes, tents, paddles, life vests, a large bear-proof food barrel, utensils for meals and a few smaller bags with medical supplies and ropes. We were forced to reduce the number of things we packed, reuse what we could, repurpose things for multiple uses and think of everything as a resource.

All of this led to the experience of a lifetime. At our pickup point at the end of our two days, the six of us walked out with only one very small bag of waste.

\* \* \*

The June 2018 *National Geographic* article on pollution makes mention of a "circular economy." I had never before heard the term, so I was intrigued. The concept of a circular economy offered me a map to a new potential destination, so understanding and following that concept became my new focus.

The main goal of a circular economy is a result of "no waste." However, at the time of my first introduction to it in 2018, "no waste" seemed highly unattainable. As I reflect back now— particularly after the canoe trip—I know that, while actuality is the ultimate goal, it seems more important to first adopt "no waste" as a mindset and embrace it wholeheartedly.

As soon as I chose the journey of education in 2018, I enrolled in an online course to better understand the concept of a circular economy. Over the next eight months, I took three courses through edX, an online platform founded by Harvard and MIT to promote learning and education by removing barriers of cost, location and access.[4] My courses included "The Circular Economy: An Introduction," "Engineering Design for a Circular Economy" and "Sustainable Packaging in a Circular Economy." Each course provided a broad context for my journey, along with countless resources to pursue. My understanding of circular and linear economies comes primarily from these three courses.

A circular economy refers to a regenerative economic system whereby waste and process by-products are turned into new inputs for new products. The regeneration at a product's end-of-life is achieved through material choice, long-lasting design, maintenance, repair, reuse, remanufacturing, recycling and composting. A circular mindset views resources as limited. Production is linked to distribution, then to consumption and finally to end-of-life. All products at end-of-life are viewed as usable raw materials and circulated back to production to begin the cycle again. There is no waste in a circular system. Reuse, recycle and compost are the three main paths.

Timberland's partnership in 2014 with tire manufacturer Omni United provides an example of circular economy. A line of tires was purposely designed to be recycled and made into Timberland footwear outsoles at the end of the tires' life cycle.[5] The Timberland and Omni partnership "upcycles" the tires. Upcycling converts recovered materials into new products of better quality and or function. Upcycling elongates the useful life of materials. Timberland and Omni's collaboration keeps the rubber material from landfills, avoids a downcycling alternative and promotes a more circular material flow.

A circular economy stands in stark contrast to a linear economy. A linear view takes materials from the earth, uses them and disposes of them. Resource extraction is followed by production, then distribution, then consumption and then waste, which finds its way to landfills or incineration or leaks into the environment. Linear thinking assumes an infinite supply of raw materials and a profit-making mindset above all else. A linear economy seems to fit much of how we view products today. The convenience of disposability combined with the low cost of many items leads to linear thinking and systems.

Even recycling can follow a linear path. Oft times, recycling recovered material turns into lower-quality or lower-functionality products, such as high-quality plastic packaging downcycled into hard plastic fencing. Downcycling still most likely leads to ultimate disposal in a landfill.

Domestic collection systems keep the linear economy and

disposable addiction hidden from public view. Weekly pickups allow garbage to become invisible, although its ill effects are long-term. Where collection systems are not found in other parts of the world, products and packaging tend to be disposed of in the natural environment. Non-collected disposal is often referred to as "leakage." Leakage is visible in our oceans and our lands. The goal of a circular economy is to eliminate leakage and all waste through closed loop systems.

Closed loop systems seek to keep resources in the economy by acquiring the product at its end-of-life, reprocessing the collected materials in some way and then re-marketing the new products to begin the cycle again. The waste from the first-generation product forms the raw materials for the next product. If any of these steps are missed, resources fall out of the economy. If we cannot collect the items, if we cannot reprocess the items or if we cannot re-market the items, we do not have a closed loop system. Without closing the loop, production becomes linear and waste winds up in landfills, incineration or the natural environment.

The concept of a circular economy has been around for decades. Since 2014, it has gained increasing momentum through a wide variety of organizations, government mandates, consumer demand and media coverage. The momentum stems from our increasing awareness of how we, as consumers, have grown to view products as disposable. From appliances to clothing to packaging, the disposable and linear way of thinking has dominated our society.

Plastic is the perfect material for a linear mindset focused on convenience. Plastic is cheap, strong, versatile and readily available and can make virtually anything. However, the Blue Planet TV program in 2017 and the cover of the June 2018 *National Geographic* both showed the wide-scale problem of disposable packaging. Disposable plastics and packaging (bottles, cups, straws, bags, eating utensils, Q-tips, etc.) have leaked into the natural environment at an increasingly alarming rate.

How did it get there? Who is doing this? What can be done?

Questions lead to more questions, but all seems to point toward adopting a circular economy. A circular economy for packaging incorporates systematic thinking on everything from design, to the raw materials we source, to how we convert those raw materials, to the end-of-life destination for the packaging. There is a tremendous opportunity for manufacturing businesses like ours to become a part of a movement toward a more sustainable, more responsible and more circular packaging system.

Understanding the concepts of circularity through online courses helped me formulate a circular mindset, but how to apply this new knowledge to our specific industry was still a mystery. In searching for more information, I came across the best map for my journey.

The Ellen McArthur Foundation is an organization dedicated to accelerating the transition to a circular economy.[6] While their focus is on the entire economy and all industries, they've published a dedicated plastics report: "The New Plastics Economy: Rethinking the Future of Plastics." This report relays the many benefits of plastics while also describing the increasingly apparent drawbacks.[7]

It became clear to me that ideally we needed to find materials we could source, manufacture and sell that had a biobased raw material feedstock and a circular end-of-life path as outlined in "The New Plastic Economy". At this point, I was not completely familiar with where to find such materials or exactly what they represented. A circular "no waste" system was still just theoretical in my mind.

However, the technology company Salesforce continuously reminds customers that businesses are the organizations best positioned to make real change. As a client, I have been to multiple Salesforce trade shows and events where this theme is restated.

So I began to think that our business could make a positive

change in how we operate and the materials we offer clients.

Also, plastic production is not going away. It is expected to double in the next twenty years and almost quadruple by 2050.[8] Meanwhile, a study across four global markets—Australia, China, the United Kingdom and the United States—has revealed that 92% of respondents feel sustainability practices should be standard business practices.[9]

So I began to think we had a responsibility to make positive change in a sustainable direction.

The Ellen MacArthur Foundation's "The New Plastics Economy" provided a map for my journey and gave me hope of solutions. I now felt like I had an oar in my boat. The largest obstacle to my path of preservation had been whether we could find enough business to provide employment and job security for our employees' families. The concept of a circular economy offered hope that this path was actually a walkable hill and not a perilous mountain.

I was becoming increasingly interested in those in our industry who were already experiencing the pressure to change. The Ellen McArthur Foundation is headquartered in England, so I began my search in Europe, thinking the issue was more acute there than in the United States.

## Chapter 3

# Experience It

### Ekoplaza in Amsterdam and the EuPC Plastic Strategy Conference in Brussels

On an autumn day in Brussels in September 2018, my wife and I were taking some time to enjoy ourselves.

While Amsterdam—where we'd been just before—had seemed free and open, Brussels, the capital of the European Union, felt a bit guarded and rigid.

Our hotel was approximately a mile from the Grand Place, to which we walked several times through both bustling city streets and narrower, more isolated medieval streets. On our final morning, we found ourselves on a deserted back street, where we spotted, outside a rear door to a large building, guards with rifles and extra rounds of ammunition draped around their shoulders. Dressed in camouflage, the armed guards seemed to be part of a military operation rather than a regular police presence. We crossed to the other side of the road and hastened our pace toward a busier street.

We also squeezed in a bike tour of Brussels. Unlike Amsterdam, where our bike tour included nineteen others, this time my wife and I were the only ones who braved the rain and showed up. Our group tour turned private, and our good fortune struck again when the sun came out for most of our ride.

We stopped at one site across the street from the Maalbeek metro station, one of the two sites of the March 22, 2016, terrorist attack on Brussels, in which thirty-two civilians were killed and over 300 people injured.[10] We paused to stare in silence at the black hole of the down ramp under the building, instinctually imagining the smoke that had poured from below and the chaos that had ensued, just two years prior. We rode on to the next site without talking.

The armed guards' readiness for action coupled with the terrorist bombing site were sobering reminders of the heightened political environment in Brussels. They also served to remind me of the seriousness of my journey toward sustainability. It began to cement in my mind that failure to act was not an option.

\* \* \*

With new knowledge from my online courses and reports, I was ready to experience the things about which I was reading.

In the March of 2018, I had learned of a "plastic-free supermarket" in Amsterdam, a stand-alone store in the Ekoplaza grocery chain. Bag bans were the only action I was aware of to mitigate the use of plastic bags in the United States. Our company had never made the thin carry-out bags found in grocery stores, so I saw the bans as a non-threat. While I did not like the negative publicity the bans triggered, the bans themselves had little impact upon our business.

However, the plastic-free supermarket in the Netherlands spoke to a much larger target. As I read about the market, it became apparent that the aim was to bring heightened awareness to the end-of-life issue of all plastic packaging. With limited recycling-stream infrastructure and, in some places, no recovery system for plastics, bags were ending up in landfills, incineration plants or, worse, the waterways and environment. The custom bags being replaced in the plastic-free supermarket in Amsterdam were the same type of bags we make. This trend in the United States could become a real threat to our business.

In thinking about the plastic-free supermarket, I began to wonder what plastic-bag converters like our business were doing about the issue in Europe. How were they moving forward in what seemed to be an increasingly powerful anti-plastic environment? Government bans seemed limited in scope, but private businesses promoting the anti-plastics narrative created a new paradigm. In looking for bag manufactures like ourselves in Europe, I found the European Plastics Converters Association (EuPC). I reached out to them for information on their strategies for addressing the narrative, and they invited me to Brussels in September for a EuPC Plastic Strategy Conference on this very topic.

With a plastic-free supermarket to visit in Amsterdam only a two-hour train ride from the conference in Brussels, I decided to make the trip to Europe, and my wife decided to join me. I thought of our trip as a glimpse into the future, since the anti-plastic trend in Europe seemed destined to make its way to the United States. My goal was to discover new adaptations of our business model for addressing the end-of-life problem with plastics. I knew from the New Plastics Economy to seek ideas for recycled content, reusability, compostability and material that might be biobased.

The city of Amsterdam is different from anyplace we had ever been. With 165 canals, 2500 house boats, over 1200 bridges connecting over seventy islands, Amsterdam is built on water, and the water theme invades almost every experience. In fact, my wife and I visited one of the oldest bars in the city, In't Aepjen pub, which dates back over 300 years and is located just a few blocks from the port. The dim lighting, high ceilings, vintage decor and large windows onto a narrow brick street set a timeless scene, with modern-day patrons the only things out of place. The bar setting befits the weary sailor of days long past come ashore for rest and drink.

If water is the most prominent of our Amsterdam memories, biking is the next. There are more bicycles in Amsterdam than city inhabitants.[11] Bikes are everywhere, and bicyclists do not wait for you to get out of their way. My wife and I jumped into the fray and took a biking tour of the city, visiting major tourist sites as we wove through the rush of people, cars and other bikes in an effort to stay with our tour group.

Amsterdam's vibe of activity, rich history and omnipresent water environment made a real connection for us between daily life and the need for preservation. The city felt like a place where circular ideas could be incubated to see if they might develop more widely. Now the opening of Ekoplaza's innovative "plastic-free" Amsterdam supermarket and alternative packaging made a lot more sense.

When we visited Ekoplaza, we found that the plastic-free supermarket was actually a small exhibition pop-up space created to maximize awareness. When the pop-up store closed, the regular Ekoplaza stores began to use the momentum to introduce plastic–free aisles. In visiting one Ekoplaza store, I found paper and compostable bag alternatives, as well as the non-use of bags whenever products allowed. "Plastic Free" signs were posted prominently and on packaging throughout the store.

The existence of a trademarked "Plastic Free" logo was an alarming find. The logo was a small black-&-white image in a rectangular cube shape, printed on packaging to provide a choice for concerned consumers.

The train ride from Amsterdam to Brussels gave me time to reflect on what I'd seen in Amsterdam. Then the day after we arrived in Brussels, I attended the EuPC Plastic Strategy Conference—the only American there.

The conference began with an overview of the current state of how plastics were becoming viewed increasingly negatively in the marketplace. Our shared dialogue on plastics had changed. What had once been a scientific discussion of the environmental impact of different packaging materials—from how they are made, to the benefits of the package, to packaging end-of-life—had become a more sensationalized view of plastic pollution. Media portrayal of plastics had made the end-of-life problem more urgent and governments more apt to act based on citizens' feelings.

A discussion followed on how recyclers and processors are caught in the middle of the new narrative. Up until 2018, there had been two choices for recyclers/processors: one choice was to invest heavily in equipment to handle sorting plastic packaging in order to produce purer bales; the other choice was to continue to sell mixed bales overseas for a small profit. Since the demand for purer bales was limited both domestically and overseas and the expense to create them high, selling mixed bales overseas made economic sense.

When China, in particular, stopped importing recycled materials in early 2018, domestic recyclers/processors were stuck. Without either the largest global market for mixed bales or the means to produce purer bales, recyclers/processors became unable to sell all their mixed bales, and recycled bales began to pile up with nowhere to go.

As explained at the conference, long-term plans for creating new markets for recycled bales offer some hope. If either governments mandate or consumers request more recycled content in their packaging, a market will develop for well-sorted plastic packaging. With higher demand for recycled product, recyclers/processors will gain the incentive to invest in equipment. And investment in equipment will help move the packaging economy in a circular direction.

During the conference break, I asked one of the presenters: "What about compostable packaging? How do you see that fitting into the future of packaging?"

The response was: "It's a red herring."

His comment made me think that, while compostable material does return to the earth in the form of heat, carbon dioxide, water and a stable soil conditioner (compost)[12] there were obvious hurdles to its wide-scale acceptance and use. I had to determine what those hurdles were.

Presenters from different countries spoke at the conference

from varied perspectives. A member of the European Parliament from Greece spoke on the regulatory aspect of strategies for addressing the anti-plastics narrative. A small food packaging business-owner from Denmark spoke of what they were currently doing to help clients identify the eco-friendliest package. The head of sustainability from Borealis, one of the largest raw material makers in Europe, presented corporate goals of making recycled content material a long-term equivalent to virgin resins. A member of the German Plastics Association emphasized design, with a guide able to weigh aspects of one option versus another in order to determine the best package in terms of cost, functionality, branding and environmental lifecycle. Speaker after speaker provided perspective, ideas and thoughts on environmentally-friendly packaging and the promotion of sustainability within companies.

When the day ended, I seemed to have more questions than answers. How could I, a small business-owner in the United States, address the narrative surrounding plastics?

Plastic is a superior material that facilitates so many aspects of our lives, yet it is clear that we have, over the past thirty years, collectively acted irresponsibly about its disposal. There seems no one answer. Every industry, every company, every country has a different perspective on turning what seems a negative into an opportunity. Each entity is challenged with finding a better solution to their own situation.

We have all viewed packaging as fulfilling the functionality of a product, providing information and branding the product. A vital piece to this view should have been incorporated years ago: packages need to be considered sustainably from the beginning. Every package needs a common ground in which cost, functionality, branding and sustainability come together. The package must serve its purpose, brand the product and also be designed in the most environmentally cost-effective way, which must include end-of-life.

My experiences at the Ekoplaza store and the EuPC Plastic Strategy Conference provided a glimpse into the future, which led me to visions of what might be coming. In my mind's eye, I saw plastic-free supermarket aisles, companies seeking other companies with authentic sustainability policies already in place, recycled content materials becoming the norm, compost bins alongside recycle bins in public areas, widespread global recycling of all materials and an overall reduction in waste.

What I had thought a threat before was now a real opportunity for change. A lot of companies were already engaged in this journey. It felt good to think about belonging to that movement.

I kept thinking about my choice back on shore. A sense of belonging on the preservation path felt collaborative and positive. A sense of belonging on the survival path felt more divisive and negative in fighting legislation against plastics. My journey now seemed more in my hands. I had an idea of where to paddle to next.

It was time to return home and share what I had learned.

# PART II

# Feedback Loops

## Chapter 4

# Any Interest?

### Pack Expo Trade Show in Chicago, IL

Our 10x10 display space blended into the sea of booths in the exhibit halls, smaller booths like ours surrounded by multinational brands with displays ten times our size. Walking the aisles of a trade show this large all day can have a hypnotic effect. Row after row of booths of packaging begin to blend together under information overload and fatigue. Our plan to differentiate our booth visually from others was likely wishful thinking. We could distinguish ourselves, among those who stopped to talk, with our sustainable information and new material options, but we felt powerless to make real positive societal change without engaging in many, many conversations.

We knew we were just a single thread in the fabric of all the packaging companies at the show. Still, one thread, if pulled, potentially affects the larger fabric.

\* \* \*

The largest packaging trade show in North America is Pack Expo International in Chicago, Illinois. Pack Expo is a four-day show that brings together 45,000 attendees and 2500 exhibitors in 1.2 million net square feet of exhibit space.[13] Our company has had a booth at this trade show since 1996. Fresh from my return from Europe and while I continued my online courses, my brother and I decided to bring samples of sustainable materials to this year's show. Our goal was to determine the interest in sustainability among our current and new clients.

My journey was no longer purely educational. Now we were seeking feedback from the marketplace. We would show new sustainable materials and information and engage in conversations. We hoped to enhance our knowledge of customer needs so we could hone our offerings.

Based on what I'd learned from the New Plastics Economy and my European trip, we displayed three different materials: compostable material, post-industrial recycled content and post-consumer recycled content.

Certified compostable material has a defined timeframe in which it will completely break down into compost, given specific conditions. Compostable material is very new in flexible packaging. While approximately four times as expensive as regular plastic, it does help solve end-of-life problems for packaging, provided the proper composting infrastructure.

Post-industrial recycled content takes waste from the raw-material manufacturer and remakes new plastic. Post-industrial material mimics virgin film to a high degree, in terms of cost and performance, but it does not help solve end-of-life problems for packaging, as most of this plastic packaging is ultimately found in the consumer waste stream.

Post-consumer recycled content takes waste from the consumer waste stream and re-purposes it for new plastic packaging. Although post-consumer materials lack clarity and cost more, strong demand for post-consumer recycled content in packaging does provide a solution to end-of-life problems.

We laid out the three sustainable materials and support documents on a table to one side of our main booth. While not fully vetted in terms of all capabilities, pricing and lead-times, the materials did show that we had options and real interest in pushing the sustainability narrative forward. Meanwhile, our main booth consisted of the traditional plastic materials we had been selling for many years.

We sought to determine customer interest on two levels: we wanted a general gauge of interest on the topic of sustainability, as those with casual interest right now might be those who pursue sustainable packaging more aggressively in the future; and we were even more interested in those willing to take immediate action.

Our idea was to start conversations about getting away from a linear economy that uses fossil fuel-based packaging. Immediate action might be potentially more expensive and/or involve some missteps and imperfections of newer materials, but a circular economy with sustainable packaging would show our responsibility toward future generations.

While very few of our conversations with visitors led to discussing our sustainable initiatives, almost everyone was interested in sharing their own experiences and thoughts. Everyone seemed to have something they needed to express, just below the surface.

One visitor had recently visited a New York City material-recovery center, and he pulled me aside to show me a video of mountains of garbage and the jungle of conveyor belts and machinery used to sort the materials. Another visitor told me about a recycler in Pennsylvania with a pilot program to allow flexible packaging to be recycled in curbside bins. Another was highly skeptical of compostable material, challenging the claim that it returns fully to the earth.

All three of these visitors—and many more—provided valuable feedback, prompting me toward further education. Visiting a material-recovery center, investigating the Pennsylvania curbside recycler and clearly documenting proof of our claims went on our growing to-do list. Overall, we found strong casual interest in sustainability, but very few ready to take immediate action.

As with any trade show, we also had visitors who wanted to sell us their products. While I appreciate their task at hand, I generally try to weed out those folks, so as to not take time away from my own potential customers. However, one salesperson caught my ear when he described a resin, a basic material extruded into plastic that his company produces from sugarcane. My mind raced to try to link this person with one of our extrusion raw-material vendors.

The plant-based resin encouraged me to think of existing scalable materials that we could bring to market with the help of our current vendors. The idea of polyethylene packaging being made from plants instead of fossil fuel seemed to fit the New Plastics Economy idea of biobased raw materials. I asked the salesperson if he sold to any of our vendors, and it turned out, surprisingly, that he sold to our largest.

In opening my mind to those I normally weed out, I found a new direction to pursue. The one person I was ready to dismiss was actually the one I needed most.

After four days, I went home from Pack Expo with three key takeaways:

1. Sustainable alternatives must perform and appear very similar to what is currently in use. If a more sustainable alternative does not serve the purpose of the existing material to the same level, the alternative will not be considered.
2. The price of more sustainable alternatives must be roughly equal to that of existing materials. A large price premium is not a highly viable option.
3. I needed to look deeper into the supply chain to find innovators with sustainable alternatives.

Pack Expo made me feel like I was not alone on my journey. This was not a personal journey just for me, but for plenty of others, as their interest could attest. I also had faith that others in our industry would join us if they were led.

There were other boats in the water.

For the time being, I had forgotten the choice of paths waiting for me on shore. I was too immersed in educating myself and gaining feedback from the marketplace. As one truly interested, I needed to find better solutions and communicate them much more effectively. Armed with my new price, aesthetics and performance takeaways and a new material to pursue, I was ready to determine how we could go about selling alternatives, as well as incorporating sustainability within our company.

## Chapter 5

# How To Move Forward

### Executive Education for Sustainability Leadership at Harvard University

I've never given much thought to the age of the Earth or what percentage of that time has included humans. However, our family trip to Yosemite Valley in Yosemite National Park in the Sierra Nevada Mountains in August 2019 captured my full attention.

Yosemite Valley is one mile wide by 7.5 miles long, a half-pipe of steep granite rock formations dating back 100 million years and stretching up to 7500 feet above sea level, with a lush green floor filled with creeks, trees and wildlife. Just down the road stand the giant sequoias of Mariposa Grove, gargantuan trees that can grow over 200 feet tall, over ninety feet in circumference and over 2000 years old.[14] Seeing and touching the rocks and trees of Yosemite brought me acute clarity on our place in time and our collective responsibility for the preservation of nature.

I have found that owning a business can be a solitary experience, as the decisions made and actions taken by the company are always the owner's responsibility. I am very grateful for my brother as my partner all these years. He has been a tremendous help in absorbing the load. However, now I was consumed by the full weight of a giant leap of faith in moving our company in a new direction. Could I really do it?

\* \* \*

In June 2018, I applied to Harvard University's Executive Education for Sustainability Leadership. The program is a five-day education on sustainability and how to incorporate it into organizations, taught at Harvard.

"Why" I was on this journey was pretty clear.

"How" to go about implementing the change I needed in order to satisfy the "why" was still unknown to me. Discovering it seemed a daunting task. Harvard's Executive Education for Sustainability Leadership advertised teaching the "how."

I had been thrilled when my application had been accepted, but I still suffered initial nerves at the prospect of this level of training. I remembered my kids' very first day of school and their nerves, excitement and wonder surfacing as we locked eyes for the last time before they stepped onto the school bus. This time, I was the nervous student, and Harvard was the vehicle to my next experience. I packed my bags and headed off to Cambridge, Massachusetts.

Sixty people from all over the world gathered that week at Harvard in a wide mix of organizations and experiences: public and private businesses, government agencies and education, healthcare and non-profit firms. From national brands like Amazon, Chick-fil-a, Gap, NASCAR, the FBI, Major League Baseball and Wynn Resort Hotels to smaller companies, we all came learn about sustainability leadership.

As I represented one of the smaller companies, my anxiety was amplified, but it subsided as I quickly realized that attendees and faculty were not there to judge. All of us had challenges to overcome in order to become sustainability change-leaders, regardless of the sizes of our organizations. The coordination and literacy challenge in multilayered large companies was as formidable as change in smaller organizations with fewer resources. We were all there to help mold our own unique paths, each move made in concert to form our own sustainability songs. What those moves would be and how to sequence them was our challenge for the week.

The faculty ranged from Harvard professors to guest speakers and lecturers, an amazing combination of participants gathered to challenge each other, learn from each other and push forward the sustainability movement, all under the Harvard brand. After analyzing thousands of successful ideas in organizations undergoing change, the program faculty outlined for us the ideas and methods that achieve the best results. Our goal was to incorporate these ideas and methods into our own organizations.

While we all heard the same information, the uniqueness of our backgrounds and businesses allowed us to apply the information in a variety of ways. What follows is my understanding and our own application of what I learned during that week.

## Sustainable Development Goals

The week started with an overview of the Sustainable Development Goals (SDGs). In 2015, the United Nations (UN) announced seventeen SDGs for all member nations to work toward achieving by 2030, acting as a global call-to-action to raise people out of poverty, protect the planet and find a healthy balance for all to live.[15] The SDGs are broad, and each has its own achievable targets. Different SDGs hold different levels of importance per nation, per industry, per company and per person. The goals of the SDGs interact in complex ways, making it imperative to view each within the context of the whole system.

These SDGs drive governments to create and implement policies. Different countries prioritize different goals, but, while the SDGs are not legally binding, every country is monitored and scored on progress. Pursuit of the SDGs steers education, businesses and the public toward change.

As I thought about a new vision for our company, I knew I wanted it to be anchored in the appropriate SDGs for our industry and country:

SDG #3 Good Health & Well Being speaks to the need to continue to invest in people.

SDG #8 Decent Work and Economic Growth, SDG #9

Industry, Innovation & Infrastructure and SDG #12 Responsible Consumption and Production provide stretch goals for building a healthy company.

SDG #13 Climate Action, #14 Life Below Water and #15 Life on Land seem most closely linked to addressing ocean plastics and reducing the linear flow of packaging to landfills.

These seven SDGs would help form the foundation for our company's new vision.

## Two Operating Networks

Organizations undergoing change toward sustainability show that successful change involves two internal organizational networks in constant play: an adaptive network and a hierarchical network.

The most successful organizations recognize the existence and utilize the benefits of both networks. The adaptive network constantly originates ideas to push the organization forward in new ways. The hierarchical network watches budgets and timeframes and keeps the organization healthy from a structural and "core business" perspective. The adaptive network aims to innovate, while the hierarchical aims to maintain command and control.[16]

Although seemingly at odds, these two networks work in harmony. Both networks are equally valuable, operating together at the right times and in the right amounts to push forward new ideas. Sustainability objectives require new directions, and these two operating networks in sync help to create change.

As a business-owner, I am in a unique position to understand these two networks in our organization. Along with my brother and our managers, I am part of the hierarchical network tied to budgets and timeframes. I am also part of the adaptive network, as new ideas are constantly coming to my mind. I know that others within our organization have ideas as well.

However, at this point, we did not have a means for

understanding how any particular idea fit within our overall system of operations, nor any way to capture ideas or allow those motivated to run with their ideas.

## Complex Systems Mapping

Answers to complex problems can often be found without considering the system in which those problems reside. However, this leads to today's answers turning into tomorrow's new problems.

We were shown a cartoon of someone on the circumference of a circle lined with towering dominoes. The figure has pushed over one domino, and half the dominoes around the circle have already fallen in succession. My mind races to what happens next: the rest of the dominoes will fall, and the last domino will ultimately fall right on the figure.[17]

This simple image relays a powerful message: every decision we make has a profound impact, likely in unforeseen ways. Once a decision is made, the dominoes begin to fall, and rash decisions can create problems down the road. We can mitigate unintended consequences by thinking in systems and creating systems maps to solve problems.[18]

A month after I returned from Harvard, we at our company created our own systems map based on the technique I learned there. At the center of our map was the problem we wanted to solve: reducing the amount of internal waste created in our manufacturing process.

With over 600,000 pounds of waste generated in order to create 7500 custom orders per year, we had a lot to reduce. On the left side we posted the causes of the problem on yellow post-it notes, and on the right we posted the effects of the problem on blue post-it notes. We brought in groups from multiple departments to brainstorm until all the causes and effects were posted. Then we began to draw arrows between notes that affected on one another. Some notes wound up with a lot of arrows, while others had fewer.

Mapping problems pushes our mental capacity beyond the norm. At first glance, it can be highly confusing to look at a complex jumbled mess of post-it notes, intersecting lines and arrows. So we focused on those post-it notes with the most arrows. Wherever the most arrows pointed, we changed the post-it note color to pink to identify it as a key cause to pursue in reducing our material waste. This left us with multiple pink notes. Some causes could be acted on immediately, while others needed more brainstorming on how to address them.

One obvious cause of waste was our material purchasing amounts and management of overages. Material makes up about 50% of our gross sales. We order raw materials for custom jobs based on estimated production scrap amounts. Lowering material purchase amounts would have a large potential impact. Our raw material purchases tended to be over-ordered to avoid the possibility of shorting the client purchase order. In so doing, we often ended up with overage above and beyond the client allowable shipping amount. Overages were either scrapped or stored in the material "graveyard" in our warehouse.

To address the material overage, we did two things: first, we simply ordered less, thereby inherently reducing the overage; second, we changed the name of our leftover material storage from "graveyard" to "material yard."

We communicated to our production staff why we were reducing order amounts, and, knowing the impact, they decided they could make some procedural changes so that less material would not short client purchase orders.

And we agreed that graveyards are where things go to die, which is in fact what was happening to our leftover material. A name change and mindset change, toward re-purposing leftover material for future orders, set in motion tremendous savings.

While our systems map is overly simplified, it has really helped us internally to focus on causes that bring the most value to solving problems. We are able to clarify decisions through mapping problems using multiple stakeholders and freedom for all to speak openly. It is easier to find consensus once the maps are complete.

We find strategic clarity through mapping the complexities. Time does not allow all our decisions to follow this extensive mapping, but at least we can consider the system around each decision, which has a profound effect on our processes and our solutions.

## Idea Flow Mapping

Once the most impactful ideas from a systems map are discovered, the ideas requiring further thought make their way to an idea flow map, and the team or individual pursuing the idea are given freedom to pursue it to scale.

The idea flow map moves the idea from inception to completion (or abortment) by bouncing back and forth between the adaptive and hierarchical networks. The map creates a traceable lifecycle for ideas, as they flow through the organization.[19]

Internally, we created a very simple version of an idea flow map on a spreadsheet, on which we darkened cells to create a megaphone shape. Ideas start on the left at the widest side of the shape and move up and down between networks to make their way, over time, to the narrow opening at the right.

Each idea gets its own spreadsheet. We track each idea and document progress below the shape where it currently sits. Idea flow maps can push ideas through very quickly, or take a long time, or be discontinued, based on potential buy-in from multiple departments, available funds and overall resources.

Our systems map revealed that lack of training was the biggest key cause to our material waste. We thought of holding a concentrated week of interactive training sessions and gaming based upon waste. All employees would partake in at least one of nine different sessions of their choosing. We called the idea "Waste Week," modeled after Discovery Channel's "Shark Week."

Waste Week entered the idea flow map at the wide side of the megaphone shape. The idea bounced back and forth between the hierarchical network, taking into account cost and lost production time, and the adaptive network, adjusting with more ideas. We looked at multiple iterations of the timing, session content and theme of the week before the idea arrived at the narrow right side of the map in its final scalable form. The idea flowed through the map like interlinking parabolas in a narrowing tube.

After four months of planning, Waste Week took place in June 2019. It was a tremendous week of awareness, education and fun, ending with a food truck providing lunch and giveaways of our company's reusable totes and an official Waste Week T-shirt for all employees.

The seeds of success for Waste Week had been sown months earlier with its idea flow map. Now we had a blueprint for developing other ideas.

## Biomimicry

The Earth has been in existence for 4.5 billion years, evolving throughout that time to survive and thrive. If those 4.5 billion years equaled one year, human existence would equal only thirty-six minutes.[20]

Biomimicry seeks to design processes and products using nature as its model. Biomimicry serves as an aspirational guide. In nature, there is no waste, as everything is a nutrient and a feedstock for another. Nature is constantly sensing the environment through countless feedback loops. So emulating nature helps us to move toward an economic system that creates conditions to fulfill the SDGs.

For example, a peacock's brilliant blue and teal feathers are created by naturally-occurring nanoscale networks that reflect specific wavelengths of light.[21] The color comes from its structure, not from dyes or potentially harmful chemicals. Can the colors in clothing, paints and packaging be based on natural structures like the peacock and avoid the toxic chemicals in some dyes today?

Tipa Corporation makes compostable materials that mimic plastic packaging. Compostable packaging reflects a natural biological lifecycle, using the analogy of an orange peel. An orange peel is a "package" for an orange, and when an orange is "opened" the package/peel can be composted and made part of the soil, in order to grow more plants. Compostability at the end-of-life ultimately metabolizes the compostable material into carbon dioxide, water and a fertilizer for plant growth (compost), which are used to grow more compostable material.[22] Thus, the cycle continues.

We need a deep paradigm shift from viewing nature as simply a source of raw materials to a source of answers for what we want to do. Thinking in these terms is a foundational mindset for any sustainable movement. In the packaging world, a biomimicry mindset is in alignment with the New Plastics Economy. Whether the packing is recyclable or compostable, all packaging viewed as a resource for making other products or packaging moves the narrative to "no waste," just as in nature.

Biomimicry makes our connection to nature real.

## Purpose-led business models

Building business strategy around a greater purpose inspires employees, vendors and clients.

The sixty of us at Harvard brainstormed at the end of the week, comparing conventional business models to purpose-led ones. Our comparison list revealed that a purpose-led model drives stronger loyalty from clients and employees, can be more efficient, has a longer-term focus, is more human in its approach, promotes innovation, is more circular in nature and is more flexible and welcoming.[23]

Purpose-led organizations fit the narrative for companies moving in a sustainable direction. Sustainability is, at least in part, about a larger purpose.

What is our company's greater purpose? Is it clearly communicated to our employees, clients and community? Is our purpose supported by authentic actions?

These are the questions our company had to answer in order to find our true mission, vision and values.

\* \* \*

Each morning during my week at Harvard, I jogged along the Charles River through the southern part of campus in the early morning fog. The autumn air was crisp and cold, and sculling boats skimmed gracefully across the river's surface in virtual silence. The dew on the grass glistened in the first bits of sunlight making their way through the trees, and shadows emerged on the riverbank trail as the light of a new day rose above the horizon.

The uniqueness of this experience tied in tightly with our education mission to preserve the air, water and land. The week provided a more robust lattice of sustainability thought and taught us how to implement change.

The personal connections I made throughout the week were an extraordinary source of inspiration, feedback and motivation. We ate together, learned together and were challenged together, forming a bond that has proved lasting. That connection touched in me a higher need for belonging. I now belong to a movement.

As I drove out of Cambridge, I thought about how I would move forward and create the "how" for which my "why" was calling. The SDGs, system thinking and mapping, idea flow maps, biomimicry and purpose-led business models were all new tools suddenly at my disposal. Raising literacy about sustainability within our business and in our clients would be an important next step. I needed to set the foundations for the products we would sell and the internal vision change I would pursue.

I was moving closer to making that choice waiting for me back on shore.

However, a deep nervousness now took root. I knew this journey would enter rough waters as I tried to move our company and clients in a more sustainable direction. Was this really a journey worth taking? Was I qualified to do this? Did I know enough to take on this role? Why would I spend time and money pursuing a new way of doing business, when our business seemed fine as is?

## Chapter 6

# It's Personal

## Faith and Business

Just off the main quad of Hamilton College, a fifteen-foot statue of Alexander Hamilton overlooks the big white double doors of the campus chapel. His long-standing vigil remains fresh in my mind even today, serving as a reminder of my foundational liberal arts education intertwined with my faith.

Every Easter throughout my childhood, our family attended sunrise service, an Easter sermon at the top of the steep hill behind the church, followed by a community breakfast. My parents would wake us at 5:30 a.m. to get us all to church in order to walk with the gathered congregation to the top by 6:15. A towering wooden cross made of two fallen limbs stood erect in a clearing on the hill above us. I always tried to stand in-line with the cross where I thought the sun would first appear.

Reverend Lazzaro began the service just before the sun peeked over the hilltop, and the sun's entrance into the service, although not unexpected, was always dramatic. As sunlight cast the shadow of the cross onto the slope, the Reverend's words seemed to carry more weight than normal, due to our reverence for the morning, the setting and the message. Once the sun had fully risen, the ceremony ended, and we all headed back down the hill to eat together.

* * *

Like many children, my siblings and I complained about going to church when we were young—although I recall always feeling better after the service. Now my wife and I are doing our best to raise our three boys in a community of faith. We try to attend church every Sunday and consider our community needs a high priority.

I enjoy church, but while I bring home the reinforcement of positive thoughts, the internal movement I've felt during service tends to get lost as I move away from Sundays. Consistently bringing faith into my everyday work life is a real challenge.

In particular, I have trouble applying lessons from Sunday to my work life. The academic and business side of me at times wrestles with my faith. My faith does not want me to make the most profit, leverage our assets to maximize our growth or get the best deal, potentially at the expense of someone else. While not always at odds, my drive to succeed in our family business and my faith can feel like a tug-of-war in which the winner is a loser and the loser a loser.

The business survival instinct of my twenty-seven years of work is powerful and generally trumps other motivations. However, for many years I developed a growing insecurity about our plastic product around the end-of-life problem. The struggle intensified as the anti-plastics narrative increased exponentially. My inner self was providing me with feedback that, up until now, I had dismissed.

This battle within me changed when I immersed myself in sustainability at work. I realized over time that sustainability is the place where faith meets business.

Business and faith do not have to be mutually exclusive. Overlaying the two disciplines of faith and business sustainability has revealed to me a commonality of purpose, purity of soul and renewed determination to reach the common good. Viewing my work through a lens of sustainability helps me to practice my faith in my daily work, and the same lens allows me to work at my job with increased faith.

## Start Now

*"Forgive us our debts as we forgive our debtors."* —Mathew 6:12

This verse helps me to remember to avoid being paralyzed by a past problem or dated transgression. Completely own up to the issue, ask for forgiveness and trust that sins will be forgiven. This verse also reminds me to forgive offenses against me and to steer away from lingering bitterness. Start each day with a fresh outlook.

*"The best time to plant a tree was twenty years ago. The next best time is today."*

This ancient Chinese proverb reminds me not to lament over not having begun our efforts toward sustainability years ago. No action is too small. Every action is positive, regardless of size. The sustainability movement is more about a thousand small things and less about one big thing.

I can start now.

## Shock Events Expose Powerful Authentic Feelings

September 16, 2001, was the Sunday after 9/11.

The church my family attends was overflowing. We were all looking for guidance. We all sought direction for our grief and shock, as the events absorbed our beings, our community, our nation and our world.

The high church attendance continued for some time. The same interest in church occurs around major holidays. On Christmas Eve, even getting to church for mass thirty minutes early does not guarantee a place to sit.

However, outside of these events, there are always plenty of seats. Our church is generally only half full. Why do people make church a top priority on special holidays and tragic events, but not on a regular basis?

Friday, Dec 10, 2017, is a date that comes with less recognition. It is the day the Blue Planet II episode came out, showing the world ocean plastics. In response, public interest rose quickly, seeking solutions to plastic waste in our waterways. Weather-related tragedies and a spike in the price of oil are two other periodic occurrences that cause great interest in sustainability. Beyond these shock events, sustainability remains a sidebar conversation.

In the public mind, faith and sustainability share the same seat at the priority table: very important when needed, but less so in the day-to-day life of modern society. The challenge is for each of us to weave them into our daily actions, thoughts and interactions. Our lasting hope is that both faith and sustainability become less isolated concepts, until they are simply a part of our normal thinking and daily experience.

## Common Good

Faith has taught me to look outward to help build our community through giving my time, treasure and talent. I find my reward through having a positive impact on another person or institution and my internal sense of doing the right thing. Giving in this way is not about seeking notoriety, fame or even compliments. In its purest form, giving is quiet, unassuming and unknown. My faith pushes me to make an impact in this way. When humanity is served by the spirit of donors, we all benefit.

Sustainability similarly looks outward to pursue the common good of clean air, clean water and a healthy land. We find our reward in making fundamental positive changes in how we interact with our environment. In many cases, this work is done quietly in the background throughout normal daily events. Our sustainable efforts build up until they become a direct substitute for day-to-day habits. When ready, this new, more sustainable method, material or mindset seamlessly takes over, moving us all in a better direction with little fanfare.

## Long Termism

*"For God so loved the world, that He gave His only Son, that whoever believes in Him should not perish but have eternal life."* — John 3:16

Perhaps the most recognized verse in the Bible, these words hit the bull's eye. This is what my faith teaches: a great sacrifice was made for those who believe, and the reward for our belief is everlasting life. Everlasting is a long-time. There is nothing short-term about true faith.

Short term thinking is a major obstacle to sustainability efforts. Many of the sustainable materials being developed today are for tomorrow's packaging world. Today they might cost more, not be as readily available or lack the infrastructure for handling their designed end-of-life.

However, a long-term view allows sustainability initiatives and materials to be formulated and grow into the systems and products of the future.

## Faith

Faith is belief in what you do not see—belief so strong that it becomes certainty. Manufacturing compostable and recyclable packaging takes some faith.

Compostable packaging follows an organic waste stream to industrial composting facilities. Recyclable materials follow a path to recovery facilities, at which they are sorted and separated in order to continue their usefulness in the circular economy.

Doubters assume that most materials wind up in landfills, so why bother trying to change?

Faith keeps the business future as its focus. Making packaging to fit the future's waste stream infrastructure hastens the adoption of the circular economy.

The short-term doubter assumes that waste is "out of sight, out of mind." This mentality has "faith" that waste "goes away" or "disappears" or "ends up wherever it is supposed to."

However, all things go somewhere. Understand disposal helps change our collective view on end-of-life options for all materials. Just as it requires thought to choose an item to buy, it requires thought to choose the end-of-life disposal for that item.

## Balance

We all wear many hats. As a husband, father of three, brother, son, friend, business-owner and community member, I am pulled by my life in multiple directions. For me, faith is the binding element. It provides flexibility to balance my occupation and family, work and fun, family and friends, our own needs and those of our community. Faith also keeps me grounded in making it all work the best I can.

Kate Raworth's book *Doughnut Economics* describes a new economic perspective that balances the basic needs of all citizens with the limits of our planet. Sustainability offers a view of business not as a purely profit-driven entity, but also as a way of providing for employees, taking responsibility for the means of manufacture and holding ourselves accountable for the products we put into the market. These all act as a counterweight to pure profitability. The needs of the company, employees and planet all converge at a balancing point.

Government laws, Non-Governmental Organizations (NGOs) and company goals typically provide a time horizon for their sustainability goals. The UN SDGs have a time horizon of 2030. This allows a "re-balance" in complying with new mandates. Laws, goals and decrees are necessary to force change on a timeline, creating a new balance toward a circular future.

## Oaths

Taking an oath invokes a greater sense of answering to a higher authority. Our solemn promise is usually understood to involve a divine witness. "So help me God" and "Almighty God" are words often found in oaths for accepting high political office and for testifying in court. Placing a hand on the Bible is also an action taken for certain oaths, to affirm one's determination to tell the truth or keep a promise. My wedding vows included the oath: "I take you for my lawful wife, to have and to hold from this day forward, for better, for worse, for richer, for poorer, in sickness and in health, until death do us part."

An oath indicates that hard times may be coming. The prophetic words helps relationships better understand the road ahead, continue through difficult times to learn, compromise, endure and ultimately thrive, with faith as the guiding light. At minimum, the oath makes it harder to quit. In its best form, an oath provides a grand perspective on the evolving riches of relationships. Twenty years after my wedding, I rarely think about my oath as simply a statement. It has become engrained in who I am, how I think and all my actions.

While less formal, a sustainable business mindset is also an oath: a contract with nature to act in a way preserving long-term health. An oath of sustainability makes the movement within real, creates urgency to act and hardens our resolve when resistance is met. Over time, the oath becomes less a declarative promise and more a springboard for meaningful action.

## Circularity

*"I came that they may have life and have it abundantly."* — John 10:10

My faith provides a circular path for living. I was born into the waters of baptism. I live my life to the fullest. I will die, but will overcome death through the resurrection—a circular path to everlasting life.

Sustainability reveals a circular path for materials. The linear track of take-make-dispose is replaced by circular thinking and systems. In a closed loop economy, continuous re-purposing gives materials perpetual life.

## It's a Choice

Faith and sustainable living are choices. Neither is about competition or doing "less bad" than another. An authentic faith and sustainability journey can only be made by taking one decision at a time in everyday choices. It is not easy. And it is not perfect. The right choices build stronger faith and enable sustainable practices to grow.

My faith and business thoughts are better aligned by viewing them through a sustainability lens. Striving for the common good, acting now, long-term thinking, maintaining a balance and making positive conscience everyday choices are common attributes to both faith and business sustainability. This connection provides me with a truer sense of self and validates my belief that I can make a difference.

Sustainable actions at work satisfy a need I've felt for many years, while simultaneously fulfilling the core beliefs I hold close.

Chapter 7

# Who Is Already Doing It?

## Sustainable Packaging Coalition Conference in Seattle, WA

One early spring day, I found myself on a guided run through Seattle, Washington. The guide, two others and I hit the pavement at 6:00 on a clear 65-degree morning. We ran along the waterfront as the sun opened its eyes on the city. Puget Sound, shimmering at my side, was already busy with mammoth container vessels and barges mingled with early morning fishing boats. The Olympic Peninsula across the Sound caught my eye, where the choppy waters transitioned to green vegetation and trees and ultimately to bright white snow-covered mountain peaks.

Once again, I saw the ocean in the beauty of my surroundings.

\* \* \*

In April 2019, I attended a week-long Sustainable Packaging Coalition (SPC) Conference in Seattle. The SPC is an organization that brings together various organizations to make packaging more sustainable. This event was a mix of interactive educational topics, off-site day trips and lectures on sustainable packaging.

Seven hundred and fifty attendees from business, government, NGOs and education gathered to push the sustainability narrative beyond reactivity into proactivity, with multiple opportunities for learning and first-hand experiences allowing each attendee to set their own agenda.

Seven valuable lessons emerged for me from this week.

### Lesson #1: It Can Be Done

The SPC conference afforded attendees the opportunity to

visit local businesses employing sustainable practices. I toured CenturyLink Field, the 72,000-seat home of the Seattle Seahawks of the National Football League and the Seattle Sounders of Major League Soccer.

Our tour leader's first comment was that there were only a few trash bins in the entire CenturyLink stadium. Instead, the stadium uses recycle bins and compost receptacles. The stadium supplies all concession and gift-store packaging, and security does not permit packaging into the venue, thus controlling waste. It is a closed loop system, which allows a high degree of oversight at disposal. At the end of stadium events, the recyclables are collected by a recycling processor, who in turn separates the waste, bales it and sells it for further production.

On the field level, just inside the tunnel where the players run out onto the field, is painted a mural entitled *Sustainability at CenturyLink Field* with the legend: "CenturyLink Field diverts an average of 96% of its waste from the landfill each year."

Cedar Grove industrial composting facility stands just outside Seattle and handles the compostable waste from CenturyLink stadium, turning it into compost. According to our tour guide, the stadium buys local organic vegetables from local farmers who sometimes use compost from Cedar Grove created from stadium compostable waste. There are some limitations to the circularity, but this is a circular economy in action.

Certain factors keep the compostable cycle to specific areas in the United States. Seattle has compost collection, a large industrial composter and public understanding of compostable items. However, most areas in the United States do not. With limited composting infrastructure and low consumer literacy as to what is and is not compostable, combined with the high cost, compostable custom packaging is seemingly still a fringe material choice, at least for now.

This does not take away from the incredible visual of the

circular economy of compostable waste at CenturyLink Stadium. As we walked through the empty stadium, my mind wandered to a vision of circularity for all waste. If the design and distribution of packaging can be controlled, then proper disposal waste streams can more easily be managed.

Can the CenturyLink Stadium model become a world model? A stretch goal, but first-hand experience of this circular economy certainly created a lasting impression on me.

## Lesson #2: Reusable, Recyclable or Compostable

These three words—reusable, recyclable, compostable—were at the forefront of virtually every session I attended. They are also the three words most used in the Ellen MacArthur Foundation's "The New Plastics Economy."

As packaging manufacturers, we must do all we can to divert packages away from landfills. Diversion from landfill can take one of three general forms:

1. Reuse: design the package to be reused over and over
2. Recycle: design the package to be recycled at the end-of-life
3. Compost: design the package to be composted at the end-of-life

Which option is best?

As with most things, it depends. For packages for which a reusable option could replace a disposable one—albeit with inconvenience for some—reusable packages are the best option. Where access to compostable facilities exists, composting becomes viable. For most other packages, recycling is likely the best option.

Designing packages with end-of-life in mind more easily allows for recovery and avoids landfills.

## Lesson #3: Don't Sacrifice Positive for Perfect

On a bus ride from one of the off-site tours in Seattle, I happened to sit next to one of the speakers from a morning session on recycled plastics. We struck up a conversation about the imperfections of the sustainability system of packaging. Recyclable or compostable printing on packaging seems meaningless if the end user is unaware or does not care about disposal and if locations for proper disposal are limited.

As we talked, we passed an enormous bronze statue that seemed entirely out of place: a sixteen-foot likeness of Russian dictator Vladimir Lenin. The backstory and controversy surrounding this statue called to mind the seeming imperfections of life, and the speaker reminded me not to wait for perfect solutions. There are no perfect solutions.

Few packaging solutions, from design to manufacture to end-of-life, are perfect paths to sustainability. There are tradeoffs. Low carbon footprint in production, such as that for flexible packaging, is separate from good end-of-life options/ recyclability, such as that for aluminum cans.[24] Tradeoffs vary by product need, distribution network, availability of raw materials and access to end-of-life waste stream options.

Moving toward positive change is the only real goal. We cannot delay acting now, even if we settle in the short-term for imperfect solutions.

## Lesson #4: Literacy / Communication

Literacy about sustainability in packaging is in its infancy. The consumer is flooded with sustainability terms, claims and marketing messages. With many options, consumers become confused as to what they are buying and what to do with packaging, once it has served its purpose.

I learned from the SPC conference to make our business message as simple, clear and authentic as possible. We must tell a story and communicate the message of the package in a way that connects with people, yet does not lead them to falsities or misrepresentations. Clear, authentic messaging is essential in a young and changing sustainable-packaging marketplace.

## Lesson #5: Focus on Demand

Most of us are familiar with the words synonymous with the sustainability movement: Reduce, Reuse and Recycle. Perhaps the most important but lesser-known word is Request.

In creating a circular flow of materials, the consumer's request for recycled packaging content "pulls" the need for recycling through the system. Brands, consumers and manufacturers of packaging need to request recycled content. When they do, they create a market for recyclables for the processors, raw material suppliers and recyclers/processors. However, without demand, there is no incentive.

While presently the overall quality of recycled-content flexible packaging is not equivalent to virgin materials, there are a lot of applications in which recycled content is a viable option. As demand grows, so will the processes and technologies to create better and better recycled-content materials.

Our goal is to someday substitute recycled content material for virgin material. With eight million tons of plastic entering the ocean each year and plastic production expected to double in the decade to come,[25] there should be no shortage of post-consumer packaging waste to recycle.

## Lesson #6: How2Recycle®

The How@Recycle® labeling system helps the end user know how to recycle packaging at the end-of-life. These labels are found on many packages in big box and grocery stores, and new labels are issued every day on packages for many major brands.

Clear labeling is the best way to enable packaging ends up in the end-of-life system for which it was designed.

## Lesson #7: Passion

The SPC conference hosted an after-hours event at the 15,000 square-foot Seattle Starbucks Reserve Roastery and Tasting Room, located nine blocks from the original 1971 Starbucks outlet. One of only five such venues in the world, the Roastery is an innovative mix of bar, event, gift store and casual space, where coffee is roasted onsite. The Roastery was awarded a LEED® Platinum certification in 2015, the highest level of certification for environmental design and construction issued by the United States Green Building Council.[26]

The Roastery mirrors the look of a micro-brewery bar and restaurant. Coffee roasters replace beer vats, and the large walk-around bar is filled with coffee mugs rather than pint glasses. Five large coffee hoppers of shiny copper, silver and glass are suspended in the middle of the bar, housing rare coffees. The high, dark wood ceiling with dim lighting gives the space an upscale modern vibe.

This coffee cathedral drips with Starbuck's passion for coffee and the connections that coffee helps foster.

At the end of the night, I found myself loading up on gifts from the gift shop, but with so many coffee choices I needed help choosing. Ken, in charge of the gift area, had just returned from another Roastery where his job was to help open the new store. Ken served me with tremendous enthusiasm and knowledge. He knew the products, he knew the Roastery, and he knew how to make people happy.

Starbuck's passion for coffee and Ken's passion for his job were infectious and inspired in me a renewed sense of enthusiasm for continuing my own journey toward sustainability.

The SPC conference shed light on so many aspects of the sustainability movement. Each attendee will apply the information differently, but we are all moving toward the same sustainable future. Just as with my Harvard experience, I found multiple paths to sustainability. Above all else, I interacted with many other business-owners and managers already surviving and thriving on the path of sustainability.

I now had all I needed: my maps, my destination, allies and mentors on the same journey, the knowledge of how to get it done and my personal passion for sustainability. I was still wary of failure, but I also knew I was not doing this for the sake of ego-driven success. I was paddling my boat because I felt a genuine connection to sustainability and the long-term future of our planet, our business, our people and my own children.

The decision was made. I now knew that the path of preservation can provide business opportunities to satisfy basic needs, give security to our employees, offer a sense of belonging to a larger movement, create personal satisfaction and build the best version of our company over the long-term. The path of survival could only offer the first two.

Headed back to shore now with my mind made up, I knew I would not choose to go down either of those paths. I would instead help those on shore — standing at the same crossroads — find their own unique boats toward sustainability.

Sustainability is not one path. Each path is as unique as a fingerprint. Those paddling their boats must learn, gain feedback and move toward sustainability in their own ways.

The sustainability path over the water fulfills the same needs as the path of preservation on shore, but with flexibility and freedom based on every unique circumstance.

I would remain in my boat.

# Part III
# Action Cycle

## Chapter 8

# Internal Authenticity

### Changing Our Company Vision

As a young boy, I was once awakened in the middle of the night by the phone ringing. I knew a call at that hour was not good news, so I snuck out of bed and peeked over the hallway bannister to my parent's bedroom door. My older brother came out and stood next to me. My father emerged from the bedroom fully dressed and was about to head downstairs when he spotted us. I asked who had called. He calmly replied, "The police."

Our factory was on fire.

My father said he did not know anything further, but he still paused with us for a moment in the midst of his urgency to leave. He assured us that everything would be all right and told us to go back to bed.

In bed, I imagined the scene when my father arrived: sirens blaring, police cars swarming, lights swirling, firefighters yelling, smoke billowing and fire raging. Tears overflowed onto my wet pillow. When I finally fell asleep, it seemed my tears had perhaps doused some of the flames.

The following day, we went to the factory to see the damage. The press room was drenched in water over the black char of the fire. My father told us that someone had broken an outside window and dropped in gasoline and a match. The police suspected it was younger kids playing a prank that had gone too far. Anger and a desire for retribution would have been legitimate reactions, but my father seemed to feel neither. Above all other emotions, he was grateful. The press room suffered serious damage, but the building as the whole was saved, and no one was hurt. He said insurance would help us recover, and we would move forward.

He has always led our business and family by example, with humility, dignity and class.

\* \* \*

I remembered my father's leadership now, as I began my attempt at an internal transformation. I had to lead by example.

Before I could engage customers with our new sustainability efforts and material options, I needed to approach our managers and employees with the concept of sustainability and set a new company-wide vision. We could not sell sustainability to our clients without internal authenticity.

I was not interested in superficial statements and action. *Cradle to Cradle* by William McDonough and Michael Braungart discusses the concept of being "less bad." While it makes us feel good to be "less bad" than others, it does not inspire the real systemic change needed to achieve "no waste."[27] Zero waste might seem a giant leap in the short term, but it could serve as a stretch goal to drive the authentic action we needed to change our business.

I was ready to begin, but I knew I could not do this alone. I needed to first raise the literacy on sustainability with our internal managers and then spread the message to the rest of the company. My guess was that our employees were most likely unsure of our future, in the anti-plastic narrative surrounding our industry.

I met multiple times with our management team, and a new vision for our business was born: Healthy Planet, Healthy People and Healthy Company. We collectively thought the word healthy was important, as it has a positive feel and offers broad meaning in each area. We decided that people are primary, so we kept it in the middle, connecting the business to the planet. We also felt that the three terms together provided a greater sense of overall purpose for our company.

Our new vision binds my grandparents, who had the courage to start the business, to my parents, who were dedicated to serving both customers and employees, and to my brother and me, whose vision now includes the health of the planet. Our vision also aligns with the seven SDGs we found most relevant to our industry.

Our website and signs posted inside our factory now state our new company vision:

- Healthy Planet: We are all connected to the planet we inhabit. Our actions in the way we manufacture and products we produce have an impact. The goal is to increasingly make our impact a positive one.
- Healthy People: The people who make up our company are our company. The people make all the difference. The goal is to strive to create employment that engages people and provides the best physical, mental and social well-being we can.
- Healthy Company: The health of our company is key to providing for employees, vendors and clients. The goal is to invest in our company to get better and ensure the health and viability moving forward.

Our new vision statement operates with our existing mission statement:

*To Help People Acquire Custom Bags*

The balance point of our new vision is the place at which all three of these goals converge. Every decision we make runs through both our new vision statement and our mission statement. If any equipment we consider buying or decision we consider making does not align with both our vision and our mission, we either change the idea or we do not partake.

A large banner of our vision, mission and values hangs in our production facility.

Our new vision emerged out of my Harvard experience and learning of the successes of purpose-led companies, as well as the SPC event and finding other business-owners following a similar vision in shaping their companies. Our new vision was finalized through our collective drive to provide stable employment for all our employees and move increasingly toward the common good.

Now, in order to support our new vision, we needed actions. Our State of the Company address in January 2019 launched a string of internal initiatives to provide authenticity to our company's sustainability movement.

## Our First Initiative

Our first initiative was to begin stocking sustainable materials. We have some control over the materials we put into the market, but we do not make our materials. We buy them in large rolls and custom print and convert them to client specifications.

In order to find sustainable materials to stock, we used three criteria in our vetting process:

1. Each new material must be able to run on our existing print presses and bag machines, with little-to-no performance or aesthetic difference
2. Each new material must be scaled so that we can re-order as we run low on inventory
3. Each new material must be "within range" cost-wise

If any new sustainable material did not satisfy all of the above, we could not consider it a stocking option.

We also looked at potential materials through a lens of "beginning to end-of-life." At creation, plastic can either be fossil fuel-based (as most plastics are now) or biobased from renewable resources like plants. At end-of-life, plastic can go to one of only four places: recycling center, composter, landfill or incineration. The last two we want to avoid altogether.

Our ideal is to design packages from renewably-sourced feedstock with end-of-life in either composting or recycling, consistent with the New Plastics Economy, the EUPC Conference, the SPC Conference and feedback from Pack Expo.

We trialed over ten materials and chose three to make available for custom orders: Post-Consumer Recycled (PCR) content, biobased Low-Density Polyethylene (LDPE) and certified compostable material. Stocking these three materials allows us to provide clients with prototypes and low-volume orders. Low-volume orders allow clients to reduce risk, grow in literacy and minimize their costs while trialing the new materials.

## Post-Consumer Recycled (PCR) Content

To make PCR content, waste is pulled from the consumer waste stream and incorporated into the making of new material. PCR plastic has little performance difference and some aesthetic difference from virgin material. As PCR content increases, clarity of the material generally decreases. In the future, the hope is the purity of recycled materials continues to improve to allow for increasing amounts of PCR content without sacrificing appearance. While it comes at a small price premium, PCR content helps drive demand for recycled materials and begins to help solve the end-of-life problem for plastics. PCR content provides a path to participate in a circular economy and combat ocean plastics through waste diversion and a path to lower emissions.[28]

## Biobased Low-Density Polyethylene (LDPE)

Plastic made from plants originates from a renewable resource. In general, plant-based plastics have a more carbon-neutral lifecycle, as the carbon exhausted into the atmosphere during production and transport is offset by the carbon absorbed by the plant used to make the material.[29] Biobased film comes at a premium cost, but it can mimic normal plastic materials in most ways, including look and function, while steering us away from fossil-fuel sources. Biobased LDPE is recyclable at the end-of-life.

## Compostable Material

Certified compostable content breaks down into water, carbon dioxide and a soil conditioner (compost) in a set timeframe, in the proper facility at the end-of-life. Third-party certification measures the material against defined composting standards in order to provide clarity to the consumer. ASTM D6400 in the United States and EN 13432 in Europe set the two primary composting standards.[30]

The material comes at a very high price premium and has some functionality restrictions. One of the speakers I met at the EuPC Conference called compostable material a "red herring." I now understood that this comment referred to the high cost, limitations in bag styles, low public literacy and limited infrastructure for disposal.

## Our Second Initiative

Our second initiative was to engage in new outreach efforts.

We recognize the existence of plastics in our environment. The low cost, convenience and versatility of plastics have resulted in its proliferation in our lives. However, lack of adequate end-of-life waste management in many parts of the world makes this an enormous global problem. We need a new mindset: viewing packaging at end-of-life as a valuable resource to re-circulate as a feedstock, in order to stop the leakage of plastics into our waterways.

The EuPC Conference in Brussels brought to my attention the importance of recognizing the problem, participating in its long-term solution and engaging in cleanup efforts. A representative from Borealis, a very large polyolefin producer in Europe, spoke of their cleanup effort through "Project Stop," an initiative in which a team of experts helps those cities in the most need to design and implement waste management systems to keep plastics out of the environment.[31]

We wanted to follow Borealis's lead in our own community in Albany, New York, albeit on a much smaller scale. So, on May 4, 2019, we participated in Riverkeeper's Hudson River Clean-up annual event.

The Hudson River forms the eastern border of Albany NY, and our manufacturing facility is four miles from the river. In April 2019, American Rivers named the Hudson River among America's most endangered rivers. Over fifty clean-up projects were organized, covering over 100 miles of river. We participated in the Corning Preserve effort in Albany, and within a few hours and within twenty yards of the river's edge, we had collected garbage bags full of trash, ranging from snack bags to glass bottles to Styrofoam trays to discarded clothing.

Our waste collection system in the United Sates is considered very good compared to other countries. This system makes it easy to dispose of items and prevent them from winding up in the environment. However, even with our system, the garbage bags of trash that we collected along the Hudson River gave evidence of more to be done. It became clear to me that, if we have trash along riverbanks even with a very good collection system, countries without such collection systems cannot help but experience the free flow of trash into their waterways.

Experiences like the Riverkeeper's Hudson River Clean-up annual event motivate us to work harder to better understand our role in packaging and waste management systems.

## Our Third Initiative

Our third initiative was to create a design guide. The book *Cradle to Cradle* brings design to the forefront, with a major emphasis upon changing design principals to consider resource origin and projects' end-of-life, avoid toxic chemicals and model designs upon nature.[32]

As new designs for sustainable packaging become available, we consider each through a filter of three questions: [33]

- Does it contribute to the larger availability of resources?
- Does it reduce waste?
- Does it reduce environmental pressures (green-house gas emissions)?

We can apply this filter to Post-Consumer Recycled content (PCR):

PCR content takes waste from the consumer waste stream and re-purposes it into plastic packaging. PCR does contribute to a larger availability of resources when compared to virgin materials, as it reuses existing materials.

PCR reduces waste, as the waste created is diverted toward new packaging.

PCR does have a lesser effect on the environment in terms of emission, as making PCR material from existing materials is less energy-intensive than using new materials.

In a circular economy, whether material is ultimately composted, recycled or reused, design becomes clearer when the end-of-life is known before package development. Better design includes avoiding toxins in the material, steering away from colored plastics, using one material type and communicating the end-of-life options on the package.

Inspired by *Cradle to Cradle* and the German Plastics Association presentation at the EuPC Conference in Brussels, our company created a design guide spreadsheet to help our clients evaluate their options for more sustainable packages. Horizontal rows on the design guide lists fourteen packaging options, including material type, material thickness, ink type, manufacturing location, labeling, material color and bag construction. Vertical columns in the design guide provide a color-coded rating for the "sustainability" of each option, in three categories: product protection, resource use emissions and circular economy end-of-life. Green indicates a better option. Yellow indicates dependence upon other factors. Red indicates the potential to do better.

We can place laminated bags on this design guide:

A laminated bag, such as a potato chip bag, is a common package found in grocery stores today. Lamination is typically a multi-material structure that helps elongate shelf life. Layers of material are "glued or "laminated" together to provide the package with aroma, moisture and grease barriers, along with sealing and print layers to form the package and inform the consumer of the contents. We give laminations a green indicator for superior product protection, as this elongates product life both before and after sale. However, many times multiple different materials are needed to make a laminated bag, and materials laminated together that follow different end-of-life waste streams are a big challenge. So we give laminations a red indicator for both resource use and end-of-life.

While there are no absolutes, our simple design guide provides some direction and offers options to our clients in designing their packaging.

## Our Fourth Initiative

Our fourth initiative was to reconsider our printing inks. We have used water-based ink for many years, a superior choice regarding emissions and hazardous waste, compared to traditional solvent-based ink. When we engaged with our ink supplier, we found they were working on a new water-based ink that replaces petrochemically-based raw materials, to the greatest degree possible, with renewable biobased ones. We will be transitioning to this new ink system, which has a superior raw material story to match its positive emissions story.

## Our Fifth Initiative

Our fifth initiative was to expand our print options. As members of the SPC, we are able to recommend to clients the How2Recycle® label on their packaging.

The How2Recycle® label clearly communicates to the consumer what to do with each package at the end-of-life, addressing the entire package. Major brands like Walmart, Nestle, Target, Hasbro, General Mill and Natures Path all increasingly use the How2Recycle® label across a wide variety of products.

We can use paper towel packaging as an example:

Paper towel packaging contains two materials besides the paper towels: cardboard dowel and plastic overwrap. The How2Recycle® label instructs the consumer to recycle the cardboard through traditional curbside pickup and recycle the plastic in an in-store collection bin.

For packaging that cannot be recycled, like a multilayer package for some snack foods, the How2Recycle® label informs the consumer that the package cannot be recycled. Identifying non-recyclable packaging is important to avoid contamination of recyclables.

End-of-life directives through printing on the package provides each package with an increased chance of remaining in the circular economy and out of the environment.

## Our Sixth Initiative

A critical initiative was to improve our communications to our current and future clients.

We developed a new sustainability page for our website, on which we state our new vision and detail our efforts and initiatives. We made a video to encourage all our clients to participate in the sustainability movement. We used social media at each step along the way to record our experiences, with nine blog posts documenting our journey. We sent email blasts to remind clients of our new sustainable options. And we enacted "double quoting" where applicable, quoting alternative "greener" options along with our quotes for clients' original requests.

With our new internal vision established and six initiatives underway, sustainability literacy and some foundational understanding of the circular economy had begun. I wanted to improve our grasp on these topics to the point where our employees would feel compelled to take action in a sustainable direction without prompting.

Now, the most encompassing and challenging initiative would be to include all employees in making organizational change, in order to truly authenticate our journey. That would take time, planning and a lot of effort. But the reward would be well worth it.

## Chapter 9

# Stretch To Authenticate

### Our Internal Vision Adoption

Lake Dunmore is a freshwater lake in the middle of Vermont, three miles long north-to-south and one mile wide. From the time I was a toddler until I was an early teenager, my family, along with seven other families, caravanned to cabins near the southern end of Lake Dunmore for a week every early July.

Just off the main road, a wide-open rectangular ten acres is carved out of the woods. The grounds are bound by the tree-lined main road, rustic cabins and a recreation hall. A tennis court, swing set, volleyball court, horseshoe pits, swimming pool and acres of open fields fill the middle, with a quarter-mile wooded path to the lakefront at the far corner. For children, it is an outdoor wonderland.

We spent our days playing ping-pong and shuffleboard in the recreation hall, swimming in the pool, fishing, playing tennis and boating on the lake. Our nights were filled with trips to town for ice cream, roasting marshmallows, playing board games, catching fireflies and running around with our friends. Our parents gave us free reign in the contained space.

Almost every afternoon, we went water-sledding and skiing. With sixteen adults and more than fifteen kids, it took all afternoon to give everyone a chance to be pulled by the boat. I was seven or eight when I graduated from the "hang on and ride zip sled" to trying to water ski.

As a young boy, I found the idea that I would actually stand up on skis by the end of the week a stretch. My failure was assured. I spent the first few days either letting go of the tow-rope handle when I leaned too far back or, worse, holding on when I leaned too far forward. Falling forward resulted in being dragged by a power boat with my head as a water plow. I would free the handle from my death grip when my instinct to hold on became overpowered by the mounting pain and sheer force of water fire-hosing into my face. Coughing and water logged, I was thankful for the life preserver as I bobbed in the lake awaiting another attempt. While the boat looped around, I already knew the question coming:

"Do you want to get into the boat?"

An agonizing contemplative moment!

The idea of quitting was countered by an unspoken expectation of success. With so many kids trying to ski, getting into the boat would disappoint both my own and my friends' collective hopes.

I failed multiple times, but kept trying, as the adults kept teaching me the proper technique. By the end of the week, all the instruction, practice and feedback seemed to come together. On the last day, I got up. The boat sped away from shore with me in tow, my arms tensed and knees wobbly, my whole body anxious to hold fast to my current position or risk crashing.

My tunnel vision onto the back of the boat saw the celebration, as everyone erupted in joy. I'd finally done it! Their smiles, the sun on my back and the wind whipping by produced a moment of profound accomplishment.

* * *

I asked one of our production managers, "What if our 2019 plant-wide goal were to reduce our internal waste by twenty-five to fifty percent?"

He looked at me, paused and calmly said, "It would cause us to act in a different way."

That is exactly what I'd hoped he would say.

What follows are our ten steps to achieving our company-wide stretch goal within one year. These steps systematically helped our onboard employees better understand and participate in a new vision of sustainability.

## Education

The first two months of our stretch goal built literacy and raised awareness:

### Step 1: Establish the Goal

Stretch goals are meant to force action toward a goal that all involved believe is worth achieving. Stretching too far can stall any action, if the goal appears unachievable. But a bar set too low quells any inspiration, if the goal requires no new thought or action. It is critical to find the right stretch goal that motivates the entire organization in order to change behavior and build success.

After meeting with our managers, we agreed upon a 25% waste-reduction goal for 2019. Waste reduction to this extent— while still making the same amount of custom product—had a potential triple positive effect: less material required, less energy consumed by the print press and machines and the time formerly used for making waste could be used for manufacturing billable product. The cascading net impact of waste reduction by 25% had a potential of saving over a half million dollars.

Our waste-reduction goal fit our new vision of Healthy Company, Healthy People and Healthy Planet. Waste reduction would enhance the profitability of our business, allow our company to invest more in our people and reduce materials and resources, thereby helping the planet.

### Step 2: Communicate the Goal

The first step toward a stretch goal is communicating it to everyone involved.

We began our journey by communicating our stretch goal and its importance to the entire company. With our destination known and the timeframe stated, getting to our goal required everyone's help.

Our State of the Company address occurs at the beginning of every February. Modeled after the US President's State of the Union address, our meeting before the entire company offers a perspective on what has occurred over the previous twelve months and provides direction on where we are going in the year to come.

Our new company vision, sustainability initiatives and, in particular, 25% waste-reduction goal were all part of our 2019 address. Our presentation explained the reasons we were engaged in the initiative, along with the potential benefits for our company, our employees and the planet.

### Step 3: Systems Mapping

Systems mapping helps provide perspective and clear paths to the solutions to complex problems.

The ideas on our waste-reduction systems map were created by employees from a wide cross-section of the company, and participation was encouraged without threat of repercussions.

Our systems map posted the causes and effects of excessive waste. Over fifty ideas boiled down to six key drivers: those causes with the most influence over the other causes. We focused on addressing those six drivers. Some of them required research before any action could take place, while others could be acted upon immediately.

Our systems map gave us ideas and direction for the year to come, offering a shared understanding and vision, in our efforts toward improvement.

### Feedback Loops

The next three months of our stretch goal were dedicated to holding daily meetings and communicating our progress, in order to act on the education we'd gained from of our systems map, as well as to respond to new information:

## Step 4: Form a Committee and Identify Champions

A committee is formed with the sole purpose of pursuing the stretch goal. The committee ideally represents different departments in order to encompass varying angles of thought.

Our committee of four represented four different departments. We met four days a week for three months, investigating the causes of waste — as identified on our systems map — and reacting to daily occurrences involving waste. We set a maximum time limit of thirty minutes per day, to avoid the urge to try to solve every issue immediately. Alleviating the need for prompt action allowed us to collect data and channel our efforts in a focused manner as we moved along.

We opened the meetings to any and all employees with ideas, and we also invited specific employees to the meetings to gain their feedback. The openness and frequency of our meetings created a free flow of ideas and began to build trust among our employees that their ideas were being heard and potentially acted upon.

A few of the same employees showed up at many of the meetings. These people quickly revealed themselves to be champions, as their interest demonstrated a passion for the process and the goal. Champions provide a turbo boost to progress. Now we had even more people thinking and acting toward our waste-reduction goal.

## Step 5: Track Progress and Communicate

Tracking progress is vital for continuing to build awareness. Simple and consistent company-wide communications keeps everyone focused on the goal and helps onboard any new employees.

Every Monday, our waste totals for the prior week were posted at the employee entrance. The communication was simple:

Goal: Less than 9000 pounds a week
Last week's total:_____

We also posted the running total by week. A quick glance let everyone see our current and historical progress. We communicated any new actions and more details pertaining to any particular week through one-page flyers.

## Action Cycles

The remainder of the year was focused on action cycles, as our education and feedback loops turned into actions toward achieving our goal:

### Step 6: Process Out the Causes

Awareness can be short lived. Initial improvements can oft times be traced to people paying closer attention to the goal in the beginning, but fading out of the process over time. "Processing out" the loss of awareness provides sustainable results.

We looked at every cause as either an equipment or a procedure problem, not a person problem. Our goal was to create processes that eliminated the chance for waste.

One of our employees stumbled upon an example of a new process. While attending our waste committee meeting, this employee talked about large orders and how they generally cause the most waste. His comment sparked an epiphany: instead of being overwhelmed trying to control exact waste for every order, we could focus our efforts on the large orders and thereby make the greatest progress toward our goal.

We made highly-detailed job setup cards for orders that we run multiple times a year and consider large in size. We trialed a few detailed job cards on a small scale. Their success in reducing waste led to scaling the detailed job card idea for multiple other items.

For select items, instead of relying solely on awareness, we now had a new process to power our waste-reduction efforts.

### Step 7: Hold a Concentrated Week of Training

Mid-year, a concentrated week of training serves as a review of what has been learned thus far and charts out navigation plans for the remaining six months. The week of training can take a variety for forms: videos, guest speakers, vendor presentations, gaming and workshops. The week finishes with rewarding everyone for the job done thus far.

Waste Week for us took place in June 2019. We had nine 30-minute sessions addressing nine different aspects of waste, and all employees were asked to sign up for at least one session. Sessions included videos on the circular economy, opportunities to learn about different departments, a waste workshop and a Jeopardy-style waste trivia game. It was a fun and enlightening week. The production time we lost paled in comparison to the education, awareness and ideas we gained. We finished the week with a food truck to feed all and T-shirts and reusable tote giveaways.

### Step 8: Maintain Over the Summer

On-going actions always continue toward the stretch goal, but generating new ideas and holding consistent meetings can take a break. This respite helps gather new energy for the final push.

Our business year tends to have four time periods, not necessarily aligned with the four seasons. January to Memorial Day is "go" time, when we institute new initiatives for the new year. Memorial Day to Labor Day is affected by vacations for employees, vendors and clients, during which period we have more to do with fewer people, generally making full engagement in additional initiatives more difficult. Labor Day to Thanksgiving is once again time to engage. And late November to the first of the year is more like summer, dominated by time-off.

Once our concentrated training week ended in June, our goal for the summer was to maintain what we had done thus far. We still posted our weekly waste totals, but otherwise we took a break, helping everyone re-charge for the fall.

## Step 9: Meet in September and Hold a Short Training in October

A re-set of the stretch goal and related actions helps re-engage everyone for the final push toward the goal. And a final short training session fuels momentum.

We met as company in early September to discuss the final four months of the year. This meeting mimicked our State of the Company address, albeit on a smaller scale. We reminded everyone of our accomplishments thus far and of our ultimate waste-reduction goal for the end of the year.

We also conducted a short waste video training session in October, which served as the final group session directing us toward our goal.

We continued our weekly posting of waste numbers. Our waste committee also continued to meet periodically, to follow up on ideas-in-progress and keep open a dialogue on new ideas. The champions in our plant remained a continuing source of action and feedback.

## Step 10: Reward Results on a Plant-Wide Basis in January

Once the process is complete, the team is rewarded.

The holidays are busy, so we rewarded our employees for the results of our 2019 goal in January 2020, when we could bring more attention to their accomplishment.

Our company did accomplish our goal of 25% reduction in waste. We are extremely grateful for the work, ingenuity and participation of all!

For the 2020 year to come, our waste-reduction initiative

will spin off into a smaller committee, continuing to pursue less waste. We will create a new stretch goal based on a new initiative, form a new committee and begin the process again. The committee that carried our waste-reduction initiative through 2019 gained valuable experience and education on what it takes to create lasting change. Now, with more people trained, multiple initiatives can take root.

In review, we found that, as 2019 unfolded, our stretch goal had a purpose-led effect on our entire company. The stretch goal, consistent meetings and plant-wide communications changed our company culture. Some employees began to act on their own to reduce waste through awareness and suggested new processes. Reducing waste was no longer only job-by-job recordkeeping, but tied each job to a larger goal that could be measured, tracked and communicated. Our plant-wide goal gave us all more energy, more direction and more purpose in working together. We began to more fully understand the systems that cause waste as we changed them.

Our reduced-waste initiative engaged the entire company. Early in the process, we struggled to find our balance in raising awareness and creating an internal movement. As we continued to try different things and gave ourselves leeway within the planned timeframe, we were able to get up on our skis and begin to move in a positive direction. That direction got us all closer to our new vision of Healthy Planet, Healthy People and Healthy Company.

Our stretch goal made our company feel more cohesive.

My boat now included others. We had to begin paddling harder. Troubled waters were ahead, as selling more sustainable packaging with some limitations at a premium cost would be a major obstacle.

It was time to sell our new vision and materials in earnest.

# Chapter 10

# Who's Buying?

## Selling Our New Vision and Materials

On our family trip to Yosemite National Park in August 2019, my wife, our three boys and I all hiked to Vernal Falls in the eastern corner of Yosemite Valley. The first mile on that hot morning was a narrow, mostly-paved trail that led to a footbridge. As we looked up the gorge from the footbridge, we saw distant falls, while along the right side of the gorge ran the trail to the top of the waterfall. We had a decision to make: either turn back, since we'd been able to see the falls from afar, or push forward on a more difficult path to what seemed a worthy goal.

Our nine-year-old was gung-ho to take up the challenge, so we crossed the footbridge to begin our ascent up Mist Trail. After a long and slow climb on the lower portion, the trail grew more strenuous, nearing the falls. Finally, we came to six hundred wet stone steps to the top. Due to the steep grade and poor footing, we encountered many hikers turning around to go back.

Mist Trail takes its name from the mist that falls on hikers climbing the slippery rocks around the massive waterfall. The mist that day intermingled with the sun's rays to form an arc of color from the top of the falls to the depths of the gorge, an enormous rainbow that caused a backup on the trail, as many stopped to take pictures.

The 1.7-mile hike ended at a wide gathering area atop Vernal Falls. Gushing water from higher elevations rushed past us and disappeared over the edge. My fear of heights peaks when I get too close to a drop-off, so I stayed back. However, my wife and sons moved as close as possible to the point where the water changes from flowing to falling.

The sun was high against a solid blue sky uninterrupted by

clouds. Steel-gray granite rock stretched to the sky on all sides, their nearly-vertical slopes peppered with forest-green pine trees growing on any available outcrop. I watched my family as they leaned toward the view of falling water and the gorge below.

I felt that powerful feeling again: the feeling of being happy, present, in tune with my surroundings and grateful for all that is. After a reflective moment, I turned to see a trail that led to even higher ground. Nevada Falls lay one mile further up.

\* \* \*

We had stocked sustainable materials, changed our company vision, trained our staff in sustainable thinking, blogged about our progress, incorporated sustainability into our website and launched internal initiatives to make our journey increasingly authentic.

We were ready for our clients to get excited.

Unfortunately, we hit a roadblock. An action cycle is continuously fed by learning and feedback. We needed to get over the three hurdles of literacy, patience and cost in order to inspire client action.

## First Hurdle: Literacy

I was increasingly asked by friends and family, "How is business now, with the bag bans and negativism surrounding single-use plastics?" I knew I had to find a definitive answer before I could spread literacy to our clients.

Bag bans have a clear target: carry-out single-use grocery bags are replaced by reusable bags.

The term "single-use" requires thought. "Single-use" is the Collins Dictionary 2018 word of the year.[34] A popular definition, used in the 2018 UN Environment report, describes single-use plastics as "plastic intended to be used only once before they are thrown away or recycled."[35]

"Multi-use" is a straightforward term: a bag can be used again and again.

"Multi-purpose" is more complex: a bag can be used for several purposes.

In general, packaging helps a product in four ways: multiple-location transports, defining product safety and nutritional, branding, ingredient and instructional information and both storage and protection. Packages are meant, first and foremost, to protect the product until use — if the product is compromised or destroyed prior to use, the environmental and potential health impact is worse than the package itself.

If some of this help has no viable reusable alternative, the package likely serves as a purposeful part of the product itself and might not be considered single-use.

The custom packaging we produce does not seem to exactly fit the definition of single-use. Packages that offer multiple uses and/or multiple purposes are likely not intended to be defined as single-use.

We can use take-out grocery bags and custom bread bags as examples:

Take-out grocery bags generally do not help define the contents or help in storage at home. The bags do help in transport and protection of the groceries in getting home safely, but a reusable bag is an easy substitute, even if potentially inconvenient for some. Because the grocery bag has viable reusable alternatives for the help it provides, a plastic take-out grocery bag is likely considered single-use.

On the other hand, custom bread bags are made and printed to specification.

The custom bread bag helps in multiple-location transports, as the bread travels from the manufacturer to a distribution center to a grocer to a consumer, who in turns brings the bagged bread home. The originator of the package (the bread maker) and the end-use destination of the package (the consumer) are unrelated, requiring multiple transportations in the chain from manufacture to consumption.

Custom printing on the bag communicates nutritionals, ingredients, branding and safety information, making the package critical to defining the product.

The bread bag allows for storage of the bread at home.

And the bag also protects the bread.

Therefore, the custom bread bag is multi-purpose. According to my analysis, because this plastic bag has no viable reusable alternatives for some of the help it provides, it is not likely considered single-use.

The merits of different material options is debatable—compostable, fossil fuel based plastic, biobased plastic, recycled content material, paper, etc., all have some positives and some potential negatives based on circumstance. However, as a package serves more purposes, the need for a package of some kind becomes hard to circumvent.

While by no means perfect, the help factors clarify what may and may not be considered single-use plastic bags. With the above in mind, I could now answer friends and family that we make packaging that helps in transport, relays information about the product, aids in storage and/or protects the product.

With my own literacy improved, it was time to turn to our clients' literacy. I am struck by the common lack of information about sustainable materials when I receive questions like these from clients:

"Do you make bags that are 100% compostable under any anaerobic or aerobic conditions? Do you make biodegradable bags that degrade in the natural environment? Are bioplastics the same as biodegradable? Why should I pay for a compostable bag when it will wind up in a landfill anyway? If I can't recycle my bags curbside, what benefit does recycling really have?"

There is a lot to unpack in these questions.

We all wish there were a low-cost, biobased material that was

100% biodegradable in a short timeframe under all conditions, which did not damage the environment during breakdown and served the purposes of transporting the product, relaying information about the product, aiding in storage of the product and protecting the product. However, at this time, I am unaware of any material that does all this.

Thus, we are left with alternatives scaled to make them available, close enough in performance to fossil fuel-based packaging and cost-effective enough to be affordable.

Landfills are essentially tombs that quarantine waste with limited access to oxygen and light, making the pace of degradation very slow. Even when degraded, landfill waste does not become compost capable of providing nutrition to organic lifeforms like plants.

However, the sustainability of a material is only as good as the supporting system in which it exists, and the infrastructure to recover compostable and recyclable packaging is limited. We have faith that this supporting infrastructure will continue to be built. Meanwhile, what are available to us now are materials containing recycled content, are recyclable and compostable materials that do not add to landfills if disposed of properly.

The word "bioplastic" is a broad term representing two independent concepts: biobased and biodegradable/compostable.

Biobased refers to the renewable original source of the content, as opposed to non-renewable fossil fuel-based content. Plants are the most prominent source for biobased materials in the current marketplace.

Biodegradable/compostable refers to how the material acts at the end-of-life. Compostability is based on chemical structure, not the original source. I use the word "compostable," as it has a defined measure for degradability and an implied action necessary for providing conditions for composting. Biodegradable does not.

In its simplest form, biodegradable means an item can

breakdown into natural materials in the environment without causing harm. The term does not imply the timing of breakdown nor any action to do so. Without a defined time or action for degradation, biodegradable plastic has limited meaning. The term can actually have a negative effect on the environment as some may be misled to thinking disposal can occur naturally without harm.

The potential harm lies in long periods of degradation. Larger plastic breaks down into smaller pieces and eventually into microplastics---less than 5mm in length. Throughout the timeline to complete breakdown, wildlife, plants, humans, food chains and ecosystems are exposed to discarded plastic in the natural world. When possible, we avoid confusion by avoiding the word or steering the conversation to compostable.

Thinking of bioplastics in terms of the beginning and end-of-life of the package clarifies the meaning of bioplastics in any context. There are four possible combinations:

1. Can a material be both biobased and compostable? Yes, and it is considered a bioplastic. The material is made either entirely or partially from plants or other renewable sources AND is also compostable at the end-of-life.
2. Can a material be biobased and not compostable? Yes, and it is considered a bioplastic. The material is made either entirely or partially from plants or other renewable sources AND is NOT compostable at the end-of-life.
3. Can a material be non-biobased and compostable? Yes, and it is considered a bioplastic. The material is made from fossil fuel-based sources or other non-renewable sources AND is compostable at the end-of-life.
4. Can a material be non-biobased and non-compostable? Yes, but it is not a bioplastic. The material is made from fossil fuel-based sources or other non-renewable sources AND is NOT compostable at the end-of-life. Many of the

existing plastic bags you see today in the market are non-biobased and non-compostable.

The four scenarios above refer to vastly different materials. Numbers 1, 2 and 3 all fit under the broad definition of "bioplastic." Number 4 does not.

The average consumer typically has neither the patience nor the know-how to understand all these concepts and options. Our hope is that, as we move forward, customer literacy continues to improve. As professionals in the plastics industry, we must do our part to educate our clients as much as possible through explanations like this, email blasts, presentations, mailings, trade shows and conversations.

An increase in consumer literacy will make societal change toward sustainable options more likely.

## Second Hurdle: Patience

The length of this explanation speaks to the second major hurdle we faced in selling more sustainable packaging: patience.

When I first immersed myself in this journey, I began reading many long and detailed reports, including the ninety-page "The New Plastics Economy." After reading it, I gave a copy to a colleague for his opinion. A few weeks later, I asked what he thought of it, and he told me he'd read the first twenty pages and stopped. He asked, "So what's the answer?" as though he wanted to skip to the end and find there all he needed to know.

Unfortunately, there is no one answer. There are a lot of answers, depending upon different situations. There is a lot of understanding to gain in order to make better choices. There is a movement to join.

Selling greener options often feels like my conversation with my colleague. The buyer is looking for a quick and easy solution to their needs, and if none is readily available, they retreat to previous choices and materials. We need patience in allowing our clients to raise their literacy. We need patience internally to continue this repeated conversation, to communicate options better and to peck out long emails in the name of education. Increased literacy and patience will hopefully lead to increased traction with the consumer.

## Third Hurdle: Cost

Cost is the third major hurdle in transitioning clients to new materials, and it is likely the biggest. As I learned at Pack Expo, a substitute material must work similarly and be identical or close in price to fossil fuel-based materials, in order to merit serious consumer consideration. Most sustainable materials are more expensive than fossil fuel-based materials, making them harder to sell. As time moves along, our hope is that costs come down as materials are scaled to higher volumes.

Requests for sustainable packaging are not the norm, so in order to generate interest we have instituted "double quoting." We quote both the original request and available sustainable alternatives to all inquiries that lend themselves to sustainable options. We have also added information about our available sustainable alternatives below our signature line on all our correspondences. This information acts as an advertisement and is our best means of keeping sustainable options on the minds of our clients.

We do receive some requests for environmentally-friendlier packaging. Such requests come from procurement, where sustainable packaging is mandated, from new designs for new packaging projects, from companies hoping to differentiate themselves and from early adopters invested in protecting the environment. As we move forward, packaging considerations will not only reflect cost, lead time, and print copy as factors for manufacture, but also material origins and end-of-life options.

We have found some small successes. In October 2019, seventeen months after I first got into my sustainability boat in May 2018, we received our first sizeable order for multiple PCR content bag sizes in high volumes from a major packaging distributor. It was a moment of great satisfaction.

We had closed the loop to create a circular economy. We had found a source for PCR material, re-purposed the material into a new form, communicated the benefits and capability of the material and found a partner to sell the custom bags. Material bound for a landfill had been collected, reprocessed and re-marketed.

The moment was fleeting, as sustainable materials remain a low percentage of our sales. This is the hardest part. Most sustainable options have limitations, which our clients struggle to overcome. Low client literacy on potential options, lack of availability of specific items and higher costs all give us a high mountain to climb.

Two professional photos hang in our office, showing a compostable bag and a PCR content bag that we manufacture, in their natural settings at end-of-life disposal. These photos provide us with a constant reminder of our goal in creating packaging with the advantages of a low-carbon footprint and a defined place at their end-of-life, completing the natural circle.

In *The Future of Packaging* by Tom Szaky, Scott Cassel introduces the idea of product stewardship.[36] As stewards of our planet, we have a responsibility for how we manufacture and the products we produce. Rather than wait for governmental mandates, we in our business have taken and will continue to take the volunteer approach, combined with our current business. Our goal over time is to make sustainable materials our clients' materials of choice.

In many ways, our hike to the top of Vernal Falls in Yosemite National Park mirrors this sustainability journey. We as a family faced a decision: either turn around or take a difficult path toward a goal. Our goal was visible from a distance, but the trail was long, largely unknown and filled with challenges.

Once on the path, the hurdles became more difficult, but the idea of turning back became unacceptable. Finally, upon completing our goal, we felt a moment of deep satisfaction, before looking to our next goal and a new path leading to a different place.

As I continue my own and our company's journey, I will continually return to the crossroads on shore to help those who feel as conflicted over sustainability as once I did. While I continue to circle back, more and more people arrive at the crossroads. My future action cycle will always include helping others find a path forward that satisfies their need to survive, while they work to preserve the planet we all share.

That way lies sustainability.

# Chapter 11

# Spread The Word

## Channels of Communication

In May 2016, my wife and I went on a two-night self-guided biking tour of southern Vermont. The tour company brought our overnight bags to each night's stay and offered emergency assistance in case it was needed. Other than that, we were on our own. The tour company met us in Brattleboro, we left our van in a paid lot and we began our journey thirty miles north toward our first night's destination.

The towns through which we meandered were full of charm. We ate in small local restaurants, browsed quaint gift stores and slept in large, historic houses converted to bed-and-breakfasts. We pedaled down the main streets of Bellow Falls, Chester and Grafton, with miles and miles of bucolic scenery between.

Each day's ride was twenty-five to thirty miles long, some of it through high traffic areas, but most of it along country backroads. Some of the rural roads were paved, while others were not. One in particular ran in a straight line for miles along a stream under a cave-like canopy of overhanging trees. The dappled light, greenery, sound of flowing water and emptiness of the road gave us a peaceful connection to our surroundings.

Only too quickly, we were back where we'd begun: the parking lot where we'd left our car 100 miles and sixty hours before. In a sense, it seemed we had never left, but we knew that the roads we'd traveled told a different story.

\* \* \*

Most of our clients are in the education phase of this process toward waste reduction. To a large extent, the sustainable materials we offer and our talk of sustainability is very new to them. Raising their literacy requires our sales and service team to act in a new way. I had to become educated, experience sustainable and go through feedback loops before I could take action. It is up to us now to provide the same process for our clients.

The United States has 30.2 million small businesses, defined by fewer than 500 employees. Small businesses comprise 99.9% of all businesses and employ 47.5% percent of the private workforce.[37] Many smaller firms lack large marketing and advertising budgets or even any marketing department at all.

We are one of those smaller firms. With a small budget and staff, we use six business-to-business channels to educate, provide an experience and offer feedback for our clients. We start with the channels with the broadest reach and are the least personal and end with the channels that are most highly focused and individualized.

## Website and Social Media

A website homepage provides a doorway for potential clients. In order for interested clients to walk through that doorway, the homepage must quickly relay what the company does and represents. Meanwhile, pushing out relevant social media posts builds interest in that doorway.

We changed our homepage to include an easily-accessible sustainability link, which leads to a page describing our macro goals, our company vision and the SDGs that most directly apply to our business. This page also lists our current initiatives and includes our micro goals.

Our company Twitter feed pushes out information and shares our experiences as they happen on our journey.

## Blast Emails

An email list of clients provides an opportunity to remind clients of existing capabilities and inform them of new developments. These communications must be interesting, relevant and quick to inform.

We use Pardot for creating and sending our blast emails. Pardot, the automated marketing platform by Salesforce, offers targeted email campaigns and lead management. We try to balance the number of our emails, sending just enough remain top-of-mind without tempting clients to opt out of receiving them. Data shows open rates for our blast emails in the range of 10-15 percent. Our Pardot emails increasingly focus on our sustainable materials and our journey toward sustainability.

## Everyday Actions

Normal everyday interactions can be useful in relaying messages.

We send over 250 emails, engage in approximately 100 phone calls and receive more than forty requests for quotes every day. We use these daily tasks and interactions as a means to inform our clients.

All our email taglines have been changed to relay our new sustainability efforts. Whenever applicable, we open conversations with clients about our sustainable options, and we include our sustainable options when we address our clients' original requests. While unsolicited, this extra effort shows our clients what is possible.

## Personal Emails

There is no business without sufficient sales. Everyone in a company is affected by sales and thereby interested in them.

Our personal emails incorporate as many employees as possible in acquiring sales. We have created email lists of clients for all our sales, purchasing and service departments. On a semi-monthly basis, each member of each department sends a personal email on a set topic to the clients on their list. All messages on a list are the same, but each one is personalized. We have found that personal emails to have a much higher open rate than blast emails. We use this channel to educate clients on the availability of our new sustainable materials and to inform them of our website links for more information.

## Targeted Sample Packs

Personal sample packs to certain key clients can be sent throughout the year.

We maintain a growing list of clients to whom we send sample packs. The sample packs allow our clients to hold and evaluate the products we make. Along with other products, the clients can now experience the sustainable materials we offer.

## Visits and Trade Shows

Meeting potential clients face-to-face provides the best means of education and feedback.

In person, we gain an understanding of our clients' needs and interests, while they determine whether we can help them. In this age of social media, texts and emails, we find that personal contact still gives us both the greatest clarity.

In our small office, we all wear a lot of hats. The six channels above are shared by our sales, purchasing and service teams. Besides everyday actions, each of us focuses on at least one other channel, and we coordinate efforts quarterly.

These channels do not need to be either expensive or time-consuming, and marketing in this way allows us to maintain a consistent presence that fits our organization. Our sustainability messaging reaches a broad audience through our website, social media and blast emails and also provides a personalized experience for our clients through daily interactions, quoting, personal emails, sample packets and trade shows and visits.

I have been in sales for twenty-seven years, and every December, as we set our messaging and goals for the year to come, it occurs to me that I'll be doing this same planning a year in the future. Like the varied roads in Vermont, the multiple channels of sustainability marketing leads us always back to the same spot, but each time in a far different place.

## Chapter 12

# Finding Sustainability

### Lost and Found

I now understand why I was never able to find sustainability before: I never knew what I was looking for.

Prior to 2018, I naïvely viewed the term "sustainability" as a buzzword meaning something to do with being "green." The words solar, wind, recycle, organic, all-natural, compostable and sustainability all represented to me a "green" movement. I grouped them together, out of ease and laziness, and considered them something either too large to act upon or too small to consider. Sustainability was lost to me in the broader green narrative.

Now my perspective has changed.

Generally defined, sustainability "meets the needs of the present without compromising the ability of the future generations to meet their own needs."[38]

However, in researching applicable specifics, I discovered that the term sustainability seems to have no consensus or actionable definition. To some, sustainability is narrowly defined in environmental terms alone. To others, sustainability is a means of ensuring the right to do business, a more ethical means to operate and an increasingly relevant source of new business opportunities. To still others, sustainability is as an outdated term in a mindset trending toward adaptability.

With societal change already occurring, some believe we will all need to "adapt" more than "sustain," as we move forward. It seems it is up to each company and individual to define sustainability, as it applies to their specific situations in the larger context of survival and preservation.

When I gather my own conclusions, here is where I find

sustainability and what it means to me, as the third-generation owner of a plastic bag manufacturing business:

## Sustainability Is Found in the SDGs

Sustainability is found in initiatives aligned with the SDGs defined by the UN in 2015. The Executive Education for Sustainability Leadership at Harvard University opened my eyes to the SDGs, and the seven SDGs we chose for our business are the foundations of our new company vision.

## Sustainability Is a Long-Term Systemic Movement

Sustainability takes time and many stakeholders, in order to achieve a more sustainable future. Governments, education, businesses, the media and NGOs must interact to establish wide-spread public literacy on sustainability and push for a path toward a better future. A societal movement toward a more circular economy requires multiple organizations, within both supply and consumption streams, to interact to eliminate waste, keep products and materials in use and regenerate natural systems. No one entity can do it alone. We are all part of a larger movement. It takes time for stakeholders to gain a high collective understanding and begin to actively engage in sustainability.

Sustainability is found in long-term systemic thinking.

## Sustainability is Good Business

Prior to beginning my journey, it seemed to me overly idealistic to expect sustainability to become engrained in a company structure. Now I know it can happen. Changing energy-use over time to renewables, offering compostable, biobased and recycled content materials to clients, promoting our use of water-based inks, committing to less waste within our production processes and recycling components of our products are all good business propositions, while increasing our sustainability.

A company's sustainability decision must be founded in a

positive business goal, or the sustainability of the company itself will be at risk. My brother and business partner of twenty-seven years has been vital to keeping our sustainability efforts in line with our business opportunities. His keen business sense and acute understanding of people and markets has allowed us as a company to balance our needs, moving in a sustainable direction that fits our business initiatives at a sensible pace.

Pursuing initiatives that make good business sense with sustainability promotes a healthy company and environment. A circular economy model also introduces a larger purpose rallying all employees. In doing good for the environment, we energize our employees with a larger sense of purpose, while securing our license to do business long-term.

Sustainability is found in a circular business mindset, as we make decisions that benefit the environment, our people and our company.

## Sustainability Requires Vulnerability

On the second night of my week at Harvard, we ate in the Harvard faculty room and then engaged in an "open mic" evening. We were asked to consider taking the floor to reveal a hidden talent or share something with the group. I regrettably did not partake. However, that night has stayed with me. Being willing to take a risk, to be open to criticism and to learn through experience is essential on this journey, and that is exactly what that night at Harvard was geared to teach us.

I felt vulnerability at the EuPC Conference in Brussels, in walking across the Harvard campus on my first day, in taking tests in online courses, in presenting new materials at Pack Expo in Chicago, in revealing our new vision to employees and clients, in admitting that my faith rarely made it much past Sundays, in tenting in bear country in the Adirondack Mountains and traversing slippery rocks up long, steep trails in Yosemite National Park.

I am by no means an expert. Learning and listening is vital to my increasing understanding.

Sustainability is found in vulnerability.

## Sustainability is Fueled by Faith

Without faith, I would not have accepted the offer to attend the conference in Belgium. I would not have trialed the biobased, PCR and compostable materials. I would not have tried to position our business on an increasingly sustainable path. I would not have believed in the circular economy. I would not have listened to the one who told me I should write a book. I would not have had the motivation to change. I would not enjoy my work as much as I do, now that my faith and work are aligned.

I took many steps along this journey with less-than-perfect information.

Every step took at least a small leap of faith.

## Sustainability's Best Model is Nature

In late August 2017, a forest fire ripped through the southern edge of Yosemite National Park. The Lodge where we stayed in the summer 2019 was evacuated, as smoke and fire approached. Thankfully, the Lodge was spared when the winds changed direction, and the fire was brought under control. The line where the fire turned was distinct and stretched to the horizon. Miles of green forest and lush mountainous terrain butted up against acres and acres of torched barren ground, blackened trees and hardened gray ash. Video of the evacuation shows the wide swath of thickening smoke blocking the sun.[39]

Contained, periodic forest fires increase the sustainability and health of forest ecosystems.[40] However, when I saw the destruction, the circularity that forest fires provide nature did not come first to my mind.

I began to think of how plastics and forest fires are similar. Both can be viewed as circular. Both have positive effects if controlled. But if left unchecked, both can cause irreparable harm.

Doing our part to accelerate the circular economy of the materials upon which we depend reduces its end-of-life drawbacks.

Sustainability is found in biomimicry.

## Sustainability Requires Change

For an established 57-year-old privately-held company, change can be challenging. Self-motivation and survival have always acted as our primary agents of change. Now the anti-plastic narrative has tapped into both.

My Harvard experience exposed me to the process of change, which requires patience, perseverance, education, trial-&-error and a lot of behind-the-scenes work. A headline might read "plastic bag company finds sustainability," but the real journey is much more complicated.

The journey toward sustainability is fraught with missteps, resistance and rejection, as our literacy and awareness become established. These are all part of the process. The key is to remain positive, knowing this *is* the process. As more of us realize how change happens, the journey toward sustainability begins to flow toward a common goal for us all.[41]

When my children first learned to ride a bike, their skinned knees, watery eyes and bruised egos made them want to quit and, in some cases, blame the bike for their failures. They did not understand the process of learning to ride—nor should they have, at that young age. Ironically, my two older sons helped our youngest son learn to ride his bike by encouraging him and helping him understand the process.

The bike analogy ran through my mind as our company changed internally toward sustainability. As we taught change to more and more employees, the process sped up. As we collectively determined our next steps, we experienced less resistance. Once understood, any goal becomes much closer to being accomplished.

Sustainability is found through teaching and understanding change.

## Sustainability Can Be Lost and Found

What is found can be lost, and what is lost can be found.

I have found sustainability in the SDGs, long-term systemic thinking, circular economy, understanding the process of change, good business decisions, vulnerability, faith and biomimicry.

However, as with losing faith, we can lose sustainability. Our sustainability mindset can wane when laws, circumstances, priorities, motivation, information or leadership change. And sustainability requires action. When lost, we must re-learn and re-experience in order to find our sustainability again and again.

We must keep finding sustainability.

## Conclusion

# What's Next?

### The Future

A few years ago, we took our family vacation in Maine's Acadia National Park. Acadia National Park has "two sides": the "busy side" around Bar Harbor, and what locals refer to as "the quiet side" on the western half of Mount Desert Island. We stayed on the quiet side and most days commuted the twenty minutes to the busy side.

Echo Lake is on the quiet side. About two miles long and a quarter-mile wide, Echo Lake is a fresh-water lake with very limited access, no boats and no residences on the coastline. We were told of a secret swimming spot about midway up the lake, so one late afternoon we descended a steep hill from the road to a large rock from which we could jump off into the depths.

My best friend and I, with his two sons and my two older boys, swam the width of the lake. The water was calm, clear and cold. We heard only our own swim strokes and a few distant birds. I remember pausing in the center of the lake to be present. I saw sun bathing the smooth water, which led to green slopes, which led to mountain peaks.

I felt a powerful connection to the water, the land and that moment with my sons and friends.

\* \* \*

Do we believe what we see, or see what we believe?[42] Do we believe plastics are harmless because they disappear into waste streams? Or do we believe plastics are harmful because we see them accumulating in our oceans?

The anti-plastic narrative has brought necessary attention to the end-of-life problem we have with plastics. Due to their low emissions, low cost, versatility and strength when compared to the alternatives, plastics proliferate in our daily lives. However, whenever applicable, the best environmental choice for any material in any situation is clearly to reduce and reuse. When packaging is needed for transport, instructions, storage, shelf life or safety, it is critical to view the package material's environmental impact in all stages of the product's lifecycle. Our hope is to move our clients' focus toward the entire lifecycle of any material we use.

My journey has taught me to see the future of a new plastics circular economy and believe that we can help make it happen. With sustainability more clearly defined and thus more easily found, I have discovered indications that we as a society are moving in the right direction of systemic change toward a circular economy.

## Investment in Material Recovery Facilities

In July 2019, we visited County Waste and Recycling in Albany. New York. We saw a maze of conveyor belts circulating and sorting incoming waste in a wide variety of ways. It was hard not to be impacted by the mountains of waste at the beginning of the process and the sorted bales at the end. Our host explained the imperfections in their system and added that they need to upgrade their equipment to handle flexible packaging in particular, which, at the time of our visit, they could not recycle.

Waste streams have changed over the last twenty years.[43] Innovations toward flexible plastics are happening faster than innovations in recovery. It has become a real challenge to run current waste streams on old equipment. Equipment traditionally used to sort and process single-stream waste is not fully capable of segregating flexible packaging, and recyclers/processors have no assurances of selling the material, once sorted. The high cost of upgrading equipment to handle flexible packaging dampens any motivation recyclers/processors might have to process flexible plastics.

At Pack Expo, one of our visitors mentioned a Pennsylvania pilot program for curbside recycling of plastic bags. Local industry leaders formed the Materials Recovery for the Future (MRFF) organization to bring flexible packaging into a circular economy. JP Mascaro & Sons recycling facility invested in advanced technology to process flexible materials with upgraded equipment, for purer bales of all types. MRFF hopes to show that flexible packaging has value and can be sorted and processed from single-stream recycling streams.[44] If successful, JP Mascaro & Sons can offer a blueprint for other recycling facilities.

## Mandated Recycled Content in Packaging

Legal mandates for minimum amounts of recycled content will drive a demand for recycled materials. Ninety-four percent of Americans support recycling. Seventy-four percent of those Americans believe recycling should be made a priority.[45] With major brands increasingly onboard and public opinion at an all-time high, the demand for recycled flexible packaging will likely increase, giving recyclers/processors a market for recycled flexible packaging bales. Legal mandates can force brand owners and manufacturers to source recycled content material and thereby increase circularity.

## Investment in World-Wide Waste Collection Systems

While eight million tons of plastic waste enter the ocean each year, many developing countries don't have well-organized means of controlling waste.[46] Plastic pollution is most prominent in developing countries with less-effective waste collection systems. The result, in many cases, is that garbage tends to pile up on land and in waterways. Therefore, investment in worldwide collection systems benefits all of us.

## Public Service Advertisements for Circularity

As a young boy, I was impressed by Iron Eyes Cody as the "Crying Indian" in the 1970s Make America Beautiful public service ads, which showed the chief rowing his canoe or looking across the landscape at pollution emanating from modern life: smoke from factories, trash on the ground and humans littering. The tear on his face was a powerful symbol of the environmental movement, which at the time focused on littering.

There is no such thing as "away." Everything ends up somewhere. And circularity gives everything a place to go.

While today's messaging might be a little different, the core of a similar campaign would be helpful. Promotion of trash as a resource could push the concept of circular economy to a broader audience, in the same way that picking up litter did for me in the 1970s.

## Leadership by Large Companies and Governments

Systemic change can be enabled most rapidly by large companies and governments. As a small manufacturer leading the charge, I face real challenges in buying materials at scale, developing new materials, marketing and driving the cost structure. Compostable Starbuck's cups, Dasani water bottles made from plants and Legos made from biobased plastics in the future[47] all show large-brand leadership.

The United Kingdom has enacted a Plastic Pact to transform 100% of plastic packaging in the UK to reusable, recyclable or compostable content by 2025.[48] As more governments and large companies take more sustainable actions, we smaller companies can more easily follow their lead.

## Environmental Measurables

Current ratios, Price-to-Earning (PE) ratios, gross domestic product, inflation and cost of goods are all common economic measurables used to evaluate the viability of a company and/

or the economic health of a country. The development and wide-spread use of measurable sustainability data would force companies and governments to include on these measurables in their evaluations.

Building the social obligation of companies into value and stock prices will elevate sustainability goals to the importance of other common metrics.

## Avoidance of "Ecologism"

In the *Upcycle,* William McDonough and Michael Braungart introduce the term "ecologism." Ecologism takes well-meaning environmental efforts to extremes. In ecologism, saving resources is all that matters, while commerce and quality of life are secondary.[49]

Examples of ecologism in packaging might be: mandating that grocers only stock items made within two hours' transportation, in order to save on transport emissions; eliminating printing ink on packages, forcing consumers to become responsible for researching product nutritional facts and safety on their own; mandating that all products be sold in bulk, in order to avoid the cost, emissions and end-of-life waste of smaller packaging.

Extreme environmental mandates, measures and dialogue likely shift the sustainability movement in reverse.

## Sustainability Fully Integrated

Sustainability seems to exist within organizations as a separate entity, with a sustainability manager or department responsible for integrating sustainable practices throughout the organization.

While this is a good start, full integration goes much further. In *Killing Sustainability,* Lawrence Heim proposes just the opposite of what his title suggests. We no longer view sustainability as an isolated subject, but rather as a part of all thoughts and processes within the organization.[50] Information Technology (IT) offers a model to follow. When modern organizations first began adopting computer and software technology, they established IT departments to handle the IT in their organizations. Over time, IT has become so integrated in most organizations that individual departments now come to IT with new proposals rather than the reverse.

This is our desire for sustainability.

## Next Generation: Circularity in Curriculum

The thought of my children gives me great hope in the next generation. When we vacation in national parks, spend time at the ocean or simply take a bike ride around our neighborhood, I see them immersed in nature. Education will lead their generation in this movement, with more urgency to protect, preserve and enhance their own and future generations.

The current linear, convenience, consumption-based mindset and corresponding design of today's packaging industry was formulated in the distant past. Our hope is that our children's generation will drive markets toward a long-term circular mindset with Life Cycle Analysis (LCA) driving packaging design.

Incorporating circular thinking, with systems and economic principals, into elementary and secondary education curriculum will help establish better lifecycle paths for all products in the future.

## Renewable Feedstock Development

Multiple renewable resources are currently in development, aimed at reducing fossil fuels as the primary source of raw materials for packaging. Bananas, corn, crab shells, hemp, lignin, fish scales, cactus, eucalyptus, seaweed and sugarcane have all been used to make flexible packaging. The extent to which these materials become common in the marketplace is entirely dependent on the scalability, availability and cost of each.

Future legislation could aid in this progress, if mandates were put in place to include a certain percentage of renewable feedstock in any package.

## Technological Help

Technology advances offer plenty of hope, as ideas are scaled.

One option, chemical recycling, broadly offers a potential circular path for hard-to-recycle items like small wrappers, laminated materials and mixed material items. Chemical recycling reduces the material package to its original monomer form, to be made into new products. Generally speaking, chemical recycling takes many different forms, is highly energy-intensive and is in its infancy in terms of a scalable option.

Another option, invisible bar codes, offers a way for mechanical recycling centers to more easily sort materials. By embedding "a microscopic change in a pattern of pixels—called an invisible bar code—on the label, software can instantly identify the package," so that it can be correctly sorted. Better sorting provides more valuable recycled bales. The adoption of this technology by brands and recycling processors depends upon scalability.[51]

Both of these new technologies represent the countless ideas in development, all moving to increase the circularity of used products in search of a new life.

## Experience it

Reading a book about the environment, exploring a website or watching TV about nature might spark an interest in action, but it likely falls short of providing a deep connection. Being immersed in the outdoors uncovers our buried feelings about our role as the caretakers and defenders of this Earth we all inhabit.

Strong feelings fuel action.

We can infer that more Americans are experiencing nature in recent years, as recreational visits to national parks are up 16% from 2013 to 2018.[52]

John Muir has been referred to as "the Father of National Parks." His books and essays on his adventures and advocacy for nature in the late 1800s and early 1900s helped form the foundation of modern environmentalism thought.

John Muir is quoted as saying, "The mountains are calling, and I must go."

We all must go.

## What if's

- What if the word "garbage" were replaced by the word "resource"?
- What if the cost of waste collection were based on weight?
- What if disposing of an item in the wrong waste stream were a fineable offense?
- What if plastic recyclable bottles were worth $2 each?
- What if we always saw ourselves as a part of nature and not apart from nature?
- What if we thought of all problems as systems?
- What if—twenty-five, fifty or 100 years from now—we were all asked by future generations about sustainable living?

The answer to all the above is, "I would care more." At this point, caring more is a choice.

In a survey of 1,000 consumers in the United States and the United Kingdom, 96% felt their own actions, such as recycling and buying ethically, could make a difference. And more than half believed that they personally could make a difference.[53]

There are more people caring.

## Finding Sustainability

*"Much will be required of everyone who has been given much. And even more will be expected of the one who has been entrusted with more."* —Luke 12:48

In the multiple conferences I've attended and speakers I've heard over the last eighteen months, leadership has been a common topic. Waiting for others to lead stops the movement toward change. Someone must lead. It's likely that you are the leader for whom we are all waiting.

The verse from Luke and this leadership theme serve as motivation for me to continue to learn, communicate and lead in whatever ways I can.

They have also helped shape my mind around what I consider "success." If success in my journey toward sustainability is defined solely by sales, I have failed in my quest to find it. The verse and leadership topic teach me otherwise. I now consider success, in large part, an individual evaluation. I consider pursuing the common good, thinking long-term and, most importantly, acting on whatever I can key aspects of success.

In the past 18 months, along with some sales of more sustainable custom items, we have reduced our manufacturing waste by over 100,000 pounds, spent time teaching circularity and systems thinking to our staff, trialed and began stocking more sustainable materials, participated in a clean-up effort along the banks of the Hudson River, invested in energy efficient equipment, changed to more renewably sourced inks, communicated our new vision and initiatives to potential clients and started to plant seeds of partnerships with customers and vendors who are seeking a better future.

While many of these efforts may not translate to dollar profits today, they do offer riches for our employees, our company and our planet in the form of purpose, hope and a license to operate in the packaging world of tomorrow.

Our thread in the sustainability fabric is a thread in the sustainability tapestry. The back of the tapestry looks knotted, disjointed and frayed, in a random mix of colors. Meanwhile, the front of the tapestry reveals an organized, beautiful and colorful design. I work our thread from the back while periodically looking at the front. This inspires me to keep moving. I also work our thread with an open mind and vulnerability, knowing that we may never fully see the full tapestry we are helping to create.

My powerful experience swimming across Echo Lake stays with me. I have felt that feeling repeatedly throughout my life. I felt it watching the sunrise from Mount Haleakala. I felt it while camping on the islands in Lake George and during sunrise service on the hill behind the church I attended as a boy. I felt it in our family trip to Yosemite National Park among the imposing rock formations, ancient waterfalls and giant sequoia trees. I felt it running along the Charles River in Cambridge, biking with my wife in Amsterdam, jogging in Seattle, canoeing in the Adirondack Mountains and water-skiing in Vermont.

This feeling can be difficult to find in daily life. However, with my faith and business aligned through sustainability, I now have a better chance of capturing it. Finding sustainability has finally allowed me to find that feeling even at work.

Children's books strike me oft times as distilled life advice and lessons in short, edible bites. Reflecting upon my journey reminds me of one of our family's favorite children's books: *Zen Shorts* by Jon Muth. One of its stories suggests that there is no good or bad luck, that luck is random and cannot be judged or prognosticated, as the concept is entirely dependent upon what happens next.[54] What matters is how we respond.

This agnosticism toward transpiring life events allows me to see opportunities more apparently and devote my energy to what *is*, as opposed to what *was*. This practice has served me well on my journey. The anti-plastic narrative is not good or bad.

It just is. We need to do all we can to understand it and be part of its solution.

The concept of a circular economy leads to a "no waste" mentality and sets the foundations for sustainable living and business models. The truth is that we can all do something to help. We can reduce ocean plastics and waste bound for landfills and incinerators by choosing recycled content and compostable materials and investing in domestic and overseas waste-management infrastructure. Businesses can move in a sustainable direction through increased literacy, systemic thinking and using nature as a guide in addressing each obstacle. Individuals who feel conflicted can look to sustainability as a means of viewing their situations more in concert with their souls.

The irony of plastics is revealed when we understand the intentions of the inventor. According to the son of the Swedish engineer Sten Gustaf Thulin, who invented plastic bags in 1959, they were meant to save the planet.[55]

Plastic bags were developed as an alternative to paper bags, whose production relied on cutting down trees. Plastic is significantly stronger than paper, which could more easily lead to reuse. Plastic bags were not made to be thrown away.

However, our disposable society began to dominate, and plastics fell right in line to support the consumer era.

Reverting to and building on the inventor's intent seems to be the present-day call to action. Plastics are strong, economical, reusable and recyclable. As plastics have evolved, we have also found out they are versatile, less energy intensive to manufacture than alternatives, can be tied to renewable resources at creation and can follow organic composting waste streams at the end. Investment in the education and circular infrastructure to support each of these attributes reveals a more sustainable path for the future of plastics.

My journey began eighteen months ago, when I left the shores of a 57-year-old family plastic manufacturing business facing an anti-plastic narrative challenge. I have searched for answers in order to move our business forward, and for the truth in order to better align my personal values with my career. I now believe that both answers and truth lie in a circular sustainable mindset, in how we manufacture and in the choices we make every day.

Our family—from my grandparents to my parents to my brother and me—has always faced challenges. There are no perfect answers. I have realized once again that life is truly about the journey and not the destination. Maybe the destination is even determined by the journey, and not the other way around.

Education has led to feedback, which has led to action. Learn, listen and act: this cycle continues over and over. There are sure to be rough waters ahead. However, navigation is becoming easier as more boats enter the water and a new generation matures, with designs and ideas that increasingly consider the environment a key stakeholder in every process.

What's next for us? We have a lot to do. My journey has a start and a middle, but I'm learning there is no end. I will turn next to a detailed study of the chemicals our company uses, energy sources we tap, emissions we create, design features we offer, new partnerships we develop and new sustainable materials available to us. I will keep learning and pushing toward sustainable practices and a circular economy, knowing that packaging is expected to double in the next twenty years.

Being part of the solution is the only solution.

If there is an overriding theme to my journey, it is that we all exist in one interconnected system of economics, faith and life. We find a balance between these systems through sustainability in both thought and action. Our resources are limited, but, like the Earth, we can still survive and thrive.

To find your own balance, look for your images, find your maps, experience your journey, commit to learning, determine others' interest, find your purpose, follow your heart, join your movement, change your vision, embrace your faith, accept your vulnerability, invest in the long-term, think in systems, communicate clearly, chase your feeling and start paddling your boat.

You will find your success as you define it.

# Epilogue

We didn't want to miss it. Making sure all three kids are accounted for is no easy task, and one we do not take lightly. It is our biggest recurring challenge, wrapped around the biggest reward of our lives. However, with things finally settled for an hour, we sped to make it in time.

Albany, New York, is set in a valley along the banks of the Hudson River. To the southwest lie the Catskill Mountains, to the north the Adirondack Mountains and to the east the Taconic Mountains. We live on the eastern side of the valley and were racing to watch the 4:30 sunset from the heights on an autumn weeknight in November.

The lookout point stands along a stretch of highway, the top of the tallest building on an even sightline with our elevation, above sweeping views of Albany below. Sunset began with the distant shadows of buildings growing larger. Darker colors in the sky pressed lighter shades to the horizon. The light of the moon intensified, and the stars were uncloaked. While the sun dropped, so did the temperature. The full circle of the sun eventually became just a bright dot, and then the day came to an end.

We were not 10,000 feet up on Mount Haleakala, and we were not on our honeymoon. But we were together, and we were in place from which we could see this miracle on any clear evening we wanted.

Now it was time to go home, make lunches, make sure homework was done and settle in for the night. It was a normal day, a good day. I watched a sunset with my wife. A powerful moment.

This is the feeling I chase.

# Acknowledgments

This book would have never been written without the encouragement of Leith Sharp. Ideas for writing swam in my mind for many years, until her comment: "regardless of what may or may not be already out there, it is important to tell your experience." I thank her for pushing me into the boat.

Many thanks to Victoria Mixon who helped me edit the book. She saw something in the original draft that I did not see. Her editing expertise, patience and suggestions transformed how my story is told and gave me an education I'll use for years to come.

Thank you to John Hunt Publishing who took a chance on a first time writer. I'll be forever indebted to you all for making a dream come true. My heartfelt thanks to all who made this happen. In particular, thank you to the publishing team: Andrew James Wells, Beccy Conway, Dominic C. James, G.L. Davies, John Hunt, Mary Flatt, Nick Welch, Sarah-Beth Watkins and Stuart Davies.

I am grateful to the people who have helped form my faith over many years: Reverend Carlo Lazzaro, Doris McKever, Margaret LeFevre, the congregation of the Nassau Reformed Church, Alan Balfoort, Father John Croghan, Brian Raiche, Father John Provost, Father Thomas Holmes and the Saint Henry's community of faith.

Basketball has always been a big part of my life, and for me the perseverance to keep trying and the joy of working hard to accomplish a common goal is largely founded in playing basketball through college. In order to write this book, I needed to draw on those lessons. My basketball coaches throughout my life will always be with me. In particular, I want to thank Paul Fiore, Gary Holtz, Tim Lange, Tom Bacher, Bob Smith, Jim Obermeyer, Bill Coen, Scott Hicks and Tom Murphy for forging those values in me.

I am thankful to all those who influenced my education at Columbia High School, Hamilton College and the University at Albany. Special thanks to Nikki Piechnik, Elizabeth Jensen and Linda Krzykowski, who each influenced me in ways they will never know.

Many of the stories in this book were created by and shared with close friends and family. I am very thankful for those memories they helped make and their influence and support throughout my life.

I am forever grateful to the many people at my business who support and contribute to the sustainability movement. In particular, Virginia Trimarchi and my brother Todd Romer have provided invaluable feedback and support.

My sister Tara has served as a source of inspiration in the way she cares for our family and all those around her. I am very thankful to have her in my life.

Fulvia and Don Strevell, my maternal grandparents, lived with us as we grew up. I saw them every day of my childhood. Their vision in starting their business and extreme generosity as grandparents will never leave my memory.

My parents Bill and Deborah Romer have raised me to try to be the best I can be and nothing more. They have always led and continue to lead by example. Thank you for being the best role models I could ever have.

Thank you to my children: Ben, Christian and Jonathan. You are the pride and joy of my life. When I could have been shooting basketball in the driveway or riding bikes with you, you afforded me the time instead to travel, think and write. I will always be with you.

Finally, thank you to my wife Melissa for your encouragement, feedback, patience and willingness to support me in pursuing this venture. My gratitude goes far beyond this book. You are a true angel and the love of my life.

# Appendix A

## Quick Guide to Simple Systems Mapping

Systems mapping increases the clarity around solutions that fit into the context of the whole. Larger problems are usually systemic problems. Apparent solutions might have unintended consequences and cause other problems, if not viewed in the larger context.

## Step 1: Assemble a group from multiple departments

Make one or multiple systems maps, with eight to ten participants per session. If using multiple maps, identify commonalities and create one representative map. Keep the group size small to maximize participation.

## Step 2: Promote psychological safety in the group

The more participants feel free to express their ideas without repercussions, the more ideas will be shared and the more buy-in will be gained over the long term.

## Step 3: Place the issue to address in the middle of a very large sheet of paper

Use a sheet at least four feet by four feet.

## Step 4: Post causes of the issue on the left

We use post-it notes.

There should be a lot of notes, as participants informally propose ideas.

Resist the urge to expand on any cause or connect the cause to any other idea when it is proposed. Just write the cause and post it.

## Step 5: Post effects of issue on the right

Use notes of one color for the causes and notes of another color for the effects. As with causes, just write each effect and post it.

## Step 6: Draw lines connecting any causes and/or effects that influence the problem or each other

Causes not only influence the problem in the center, but likely directly influence other causes and effects.

During the process of studying each note and drawing lines to the notes it influences, a jumbled mess of lines and arrows will develop.

## Step 7: Identify the key drivers and ideas

These are the notes with the most arrows pointing to them. Change the note color of these notes to a different color, in order to identify them as drivers.

## Step 8: Begin to act on the drivers

Use idea flow maps or, if the driver is straightforward, implement the change immediately.

## Step 9: Keep the systems map on display

A systems map is a continuing source of ideas developed collectively.

# Appendix B

## Quick Guide to Achieving Plant-Wide Stretch Goals in One Year

**Education:** The first few months of a stretch goal build literacy and raise awareness:

Step 1: Establish the Goal

Step 2: Communicate the Goal

Step 3: Systems Mapping

**Feedback Loops:** The next three months of a stretch goal are dedicated to holding daily meetings and communicating progress, in order to act on the education gained from of the systems map, as well as responding to new information:

Step 4: Form a Committee and Identify Champions

Step 5: Track Progress and Communicate

**Action Cycle:** The remainder of the year is focused on action cycles, as education and feedback loops turn into actions toward achieving the goal.

Step 6: Process Out the Causes

Step 7: Hold a Concentrated Week of Training

Step 8: Maintain Over the Summer

Step 9: Meet in September and Hold a Short Training in October

Step 10: Reward Results on a Plant-Wide Basis in January

# Appendix C

## Quick Guide to Designing Sustainable Packages

The questions below serve to prompt thought and drive discussion toward more sustainable packaging. The optimal package for each application is dependent on many interactions in complex ways. There is no one package that is best for all.

- Is a package needed? Reduce (or do not use at all), if possible.
- What is the thickness of the package? If reuse is the end goal, a thicker package is likely needed. If the end goal is to lighten the weight to save resources and recycle at the end-of-life, a thinner package is preferable.
- What resources does the package derive from? Does the package originate from fossil fuels? Renewable or recycled sources are more sustainable.
- Does the package have mixed material construction? Single-material constructions are easier to recycle.
- What is the end-of-life path for the package? Design with the end in mind. To avoid landfills, packages can follow either an organic waste stream (compostable material) or a recycling waste stream.
- What inks are used for printing? Water-based inks derived from renewable resources minimize the environmental impact.
- Where is the package being manufactured? Local and regional manufacturing minimizes transportation and the use of resources.
- Does the package inform how to dispose? Printing how to dispose of the package increases the likelihood that the package remains in the circular economy.
- What color is the package? Clear material is easier to

recycle than colored.

- What quantity is needed? If lower volumes are needed, find low-volume producers. Over-ordering to meet minimums can result in resource waste. Lower volume also offers a lower risk in trialing newer materials.
- What are the pack-outs? Bulk packaging saves resources.
- What is the supply chain? Do the companies in the supply chain engage in sustainable practices?
- To what extent does the package need to protect the product? Packaging must protect the product until use. If the product is damaged due to poor packaging, the loss of resources in making the product itself is worse than the potential impact of the package.

# End Notes

1 Conway Center for Family Business, "Family Business Facts," www.familybusinesscenter.com/resources/family-business-facts/, (accessed July 2019)

2 Laura Parker, "We Made it. We depend on it. We're drowning in it. Plastic," *National Geographic*, June 2018, p. 40.

3 United Nations Environment, ""Our Planet is Drowning in Plastic Pollution," 2018, https://www.unenvironment.org/interactive/beat-plastic-pollution/ (accessed Dec 2019)

4 edX. "About edX: Our Story," https://www.edx.org/about-us (accessed July 2019)

5 Mike Hower, "Timberland retreads old tires as new shoes," *GreenBiz,* Nov 3, 2014, www.greenbiz.com/article/timberland-giving-old-tires-new-treads-new-shoes (accessed Apr 2019)

6 Ellen MacArthur Foundation, "Mission," www.ellenmacarthurfoundation.org/our-story/mission (accessed May 2019)

7 Ellen MacArthur Foundation, *The New Plastics Economy: Rethinking the Future of Plastics*, 2016 report, https://www.newplasticseconomy.org/about/publications/report-2016, p. 17 (accessed June 2019)

8 Ellen MacArthur Foundation, *The New Plastics Economy: Rethinking the Future of Plastics*, 2016 report, https://www.newplasticseconomy.org/about/publications/report-2016, p. 24 (accessed June 2019)

9 Ashley Tan, "From plogging to veganism: Is sustainability the new normal for consumers?" *Eco-Business,* Oct 2018, https://www.eco-business.com/news/from-plogging-to-veganism-is-sustainability-the-new-normal-for-consumers/ (accessed May 2019)

10 BBC News, "Brussels explosions: What we know about airport and metro attacks," Apr 9, 2016, https://www.bbc.com/

news/world-europe-35869985 (accessed Oct 2019)

11  Charlie Osborne, "In Amsterdam, there are more bicycles than people," *ZDNET*, June 25, 2013, www.zdnet.com/article/in-amsterdam-there-are-more-bicycles-than-people/ (accessed May 2019)

12  Biodegradable Products Institute, "Zero Waste: Composting," www.bpiworld.org/Composting (accessed Oct 2019)

13  Pack Expo International, "Overview," www.packexpointernational.com/overview (accessed July 2019)

14  National Park Service, "Yosemite," Nps.gov, https://www.nps.gov/yose/index.htm (accessed Aug 2019)

15  Sustainable Development Goals Knowledge Platform, "SDGS," https://sustainabledevelopment.un.org/sdgs (accessed Aug 2019)

16  Leith Sharp, "The Agility Imperative" (presentation, The Executive Education for Sustainability Leadership at Harvard University Cambridge, MA, Nov 6, 2018)

17  Joe Hsueh, "Systems Mapping for Systems Change" (presentation, The Executive Education for Sustainability Leadership at Harvard University Cambridge, MA, Nov 7, 2018)

18  Joe Hsueh, "Systems Mapping for Systems Change" (presentation, The Executive Education for Sustainability Leadership at Harvard University Cambridge, MA, Nov 7, 2018)

19  Leith Sharp, "The Agility Imperative" (presentation, The Executive Education for Sustainability Leadership at Harvard University Cambridge, MA, Nov 6, 2018)

20  Danya Baumeister, "Biomimicry 3.8" (presentation, The Executive Education for Sustainability Leadership at Harvard University Cambridge, MA, Nov 8, 2018)

21  Leah Burrows, "A new technique for structural color, inspired by birds," *Harvard School of Engineering and Applied Sciences*, Nov 22, 2016, https://www.seas.harvard.edu/news/2016/11/new-technique-for-structural-color-inspired-by-birds (accessed Aug 2019)

22  Tipa Corp, "Products," https://tipa-corp.com/about-2/overview/ (accessed May 2019)

23  Tatjana Kazakova, "When Purpose Drives Business Development" (presentation, The Executive Education for Sustainability Leadership at Harvard University Cambridge, MA, Nov 6, 2018)

24  Kelley Cramer & Kristi Hansen, "Just one word: Films" (presentation, Sustainable Packaging Coalition Impact 2019 Conference, Seattle, Washington, Apr 3, 2019)

25  Ocean Conservancy, "The Problem with Plastics," https://oceanconservancy.org/trash-free-seas/plastics-in-the-ocean/ (accessed July 2019)

26  Starbucks' Stories and News, "Starbucks Roastery Earns LEED Platinum Certification," Nov 2015, https://stories.starbucks.com/stories/2015/starbucks-platinum-certification-for-roastery-and-2016-goals/ (accessed Oct 2019)

27  William McDonough and Michael Braungart, *Cradle to Cradle* (New York: North Point Press, 2002), p 66-67.

28  Ellen MacArthur Foundation, *Complete the Picture, How the Circular Economy Tackles Climate Change,* Sept 2019 report, www.ellenmacarthurfoundation.org/publications/completing-the-picture-climate-change, p. 24 (accessed Oct 2019)

29  European Bioplastics, "Environmental benefits of bioplastics," https://www.european-bioplastics.org/bioplastics/environment/ (accessed Nov 2019)

30  Biobag, "About: Certifications and Testing," http://biobagusa.com/about-biobag-2/certifications/ (accessed Oct 21, 2019)

31  Project STOP, "About," www.stopoceanplastics.com/about/ (accessed Feb 2019)

32  William McDonough and Michael Braungart, *Cradle to Cradle* (New York: North Point Press, 2002), p 5-6

33  eDX, "Engineering Design," https://www.edx.org (accessed Winter 2019)

34  Collins Dictionary, "Word of the Year 2018," https://www.

collinsdictionary.com/word-lovers-blog/new/etymology-corner-collins-word-of-the-year-2018,449,HCB.html (accessed July 2019)

35  United Nations Environment Programme, *Single-use plastics: A roadmap for sustainability,* 2018, https://www.unenvironment.org/resources/report/single-use-plastics-roadmap-sustainability, page 2 (access June 2019)

36  Tom Szaky, *The Future of Packaging* (Berret-Koehler Publishers: CA, 2019), p 64

37  US Small Business Administration Office of Advocacy, "2018 Small Business Profile," 2018, https://www.sba.gov/sites/default/files/advocacy/2018-Small-Business-Profiles-US.pdf (accessed Dec 2019)

38  International Institute for Sustainable Development, "Sustainable Development," https://www.iisd.org/topic/sustainable-development (accessed Oct 2019)

39  Mark Evan Smith, "Tenaya Lodge evacuated as Railroad Fire roars through Fish Camp," *Sierra Star,* Aug 29, 2017, https://www.sierrastar.com/news/local/article170067757.html (accessed November 2019)

40  Green Tumble, "The Ecological Importance of Forest Fires," Apr 2016, https://greentumble.com/the-ecological-importance-of-forest-fires/ (accessed November 2019)

41  Leith Sharp, "Sustainability Leadership: A North Star for the 21st Century" (presentation, The Executive Education for Sustainability Leadership at Harvard University Cambridge, MA, Nov 5, 2018)

42  Alan Griff, "Trying to understand 'plastiphobia'," *Plastics News,* July 1, 2019, https://www.plasticsnews.com/mailbag/trying-understand-plastiphobia (accessed Aug 2019)

43  United State Environmental Protection Agency, "Facts and Figures about Materials, Waste and Recycling," https://www.epa.gov/facts-and-figures-about-materials-waste-and-recycling/national-overview-facts-and-figures-materials (ac-

cessed Oct 2019)

44    Materials Recovery For the Future, "Home," https://www.
materialsrecoveryforthefuture.com/ (accessed Oct 21, 2019)

45    The Northeast Recycling Council, "MRF Pilot & Flexible
Packaging," webinar, Nov 2018, recycle.com/nerc-webinar-
mrf-pilot/ (accessed Feb 2019)

46    Laure Parker, "The world's plastic pollution crisis explained,"
*National Geographic*, June 7, 2019, https://www.nationalgeo-
graphic.com/environment/habitats/plastic-pollution/#close,
(accessed Oct 2019)

47    Alex Barrett, "Lego Goes For Biobased Plastics Instead of
Biodegradable and Recycling," *Bioplastic News*, Dec 2018,
https://bioplasticsnews.com/2018/12/09/lego-goes-for-
biobased-plastics-instead-of-biodegradable-and-recycling/
(accessed March 2019)

48    Wrap, "UK Plastic Pact," www.wrap.org.uk/content/the-uk-
plastics-pact (accessed Jan 2019)

49    William McDonough and Michael Braungart, *The Upcycle*
(New York, North Point Press, 2012), p. 29-30

50    Lawrence M Heim, *Killing Sustainability* (Lawrence M Heim
Amazon self-pub, 2019), p. 144

51    Alex Barret, "Invisible Bar Codes to Improve Recycling,"
*Bioplastics News*, Dec 17, 2019, https://bioplasticsnews.
com/2019/12/17/invisible-bar-codes-recycling/ (accessed Dec
2019)

52    National Park Service, "Visitation Numbers," 2018, https://
www.nps.gov/aboutus/visitation-numbers.htm    (accessed
Dec 2019)

53    Solitaire Townsend, "88% of Consumers Want You To Help
Them Make A Difference," *Forbes* Nov 21, 2018, https://www.
forbes.com/sites/solitairetownsend/2018/11/21/consumers-
want-you-to-help-them-make-a-difference/#672cac826954
(accessed Dec 2019)

54    Jon J Muth, *Zen Shorts* (Singapore, Caldecott Honor, 2005)

55   Phoebe Weston, "Plastic Bags were created to save the planet, inventor's son says," *Independent,* Oct 17, 2019, https://www.independent.co.uk/environment/plastic-bags-pollution-paper-cotton-tote-bags-environment-a9159731.html   (accessed Jan 2020)

# References

Barrett, Alex. "Lego Goes for Biobased Plastics Instead of Biodegradable and Recycling." *Bioplastics News* Dec 2018. https://bioplasticsnews.com/2018/12/09/lego-goes-for-biobased-plastics-instead-of-biodegradable-and-recycling/ (accessed Jan 2019)

"Invisible Bar Codes to Improve Recycling," *Bioplastics News,* Dec 17, 2019, https://bioplasticsnews.com/2019/12/17/invisible-bar-codes-recycling/ (accessed Dec 2019)

Baxter, Mike. "Plastic Recycling Update." Presentation at EuPC conference Plastic Packaging and the EU Plastics Strategy, Brussels, Belgium, Sept 25, 2018.

Baumeister, Danya and Miller, Nicole Hagerman. "Biomimicry 3.8." Presentation at Harvard University Executive Education for Sustainability Leadership, Cambridge, MA, Nov 5-9, 2018.

BBC News, "Brussels explosions: What we know about airport and metro attacks," April 9, 2016, https://www.bbc.com/news/world-europe-35869985 (accessed October 2019)

Biobag, "About: Certifications and Testing," http://biobagusa.com/about-biobag-2/certifications/ (accessed 10/21/19)

Biodegradable Products Institute, "Zero Waste: Composting", www.bpiworld.org/Composting (accessed October 2019)

Brandt, Bernd. "Product Protection versus recyclability— Aspects of sustainable packaging." Presentation at EuPC conference Plastic Packaging and the EU Plastics Strategy, Brussels, Belgium, Sept 25, 2018.

British Plastics Federation. *Plastics: A Vision for a Circular Economy,* 2018. https://www.bpf.co.uk/vision/default.aspx (accessed Dec 2018)

Burrows, Leah. "A new technique for structural color, inspired by birds," *Harvard School of Engineering and Applied Sciences,* November 22, 2016, https://www.seas.harvard.edu/

news/2016/11/new-technique-for-structural-color-inspired-by-birds (accessed August 2019)

Collins Dictionary, "Word of the Year 2018," www.collinsdictionary.com/us/woty (accessed July 2019)

Conway Center for Family Business, "Family Business Facts," www.familybusinesscenter.com/resources/family-business-facts/ (accessed July 2019)

Caliendo, Heather. "Trash as Value: Turing Ocean Waste into Viable Products." *Plastics Technology,* July 2018.

Ciacca, Chris. "UN expert warns of 'climate apartheid' which will divide rich and poor." *Fox News,* June 2019. https://nypost.com/2019/06/27/un-expert-warns-of-climate-apartheid-which-will-divide-rich-and-poor/ (accessed July 2019)

Coyne, John. "Realizing a circular economy in Canada through a harmonized approach to extended producer responsibility." Presentation at Sustainable Packaging Coalition Impact 2019 Conference, Seattle, Washington, April 1-4, 2019.

Cramer, Kelley & Hansen, Kristi. "Just one word: Films." Presentation at Sustainable Packaging Coalition Impact 2019 Conference, Seattle, Washington, April 1-4, 2019.

Dreizen, Charlotte. "Workshop: The Essentials of Compostable Packaging." Presentation at Sustainable Packaging Coalition Impact 2019 Conference, Seattle, Washington, April 1-4, 2019.

Dweck, Carol. "A Summary of the Two Mindsets and The Power of Believing You Can Improve." *Farnam Street Blog,* 2015. https://fs.blog/2015/03/carol-dweck-mindset/ (accessed Feb 2019)

edie.net. *Achieving the sustainable development goals: A blueprint for business leadership.* 2018. www.edie.net/downloads/Achieving-the-Sustainable-Development-Goals-A-Blueprint-for-Business-Leadership/304 (accessed Dec 2018)

edX online course. "Circular Economy: An Introduction." Accessed Fall 2018. https://www.edX.org

"Engineering Design for a Circular Economy." Accessed Winter

2019. https://www.edX.org

"Sustainable Packaging in a Circular Economy." Accessed Spring 2019. https://www.edX.org

Eccles, Robert, & Miller Perkins, Kathleen, & Serafeim, George. "How to Become a Sustainable Company." *MIT Sloan Management Review*, Vol 53 No 4 p. 43-50, Summer 2012. https://sloanreview.mit.edu/article/how-to-become-a-sustainable-company/ (accessed April 2019)

Ellen MacArthur Foundation. *The New Plastics Economy, Rethinking the Future of Plastics*. 2016. https://www.newplasticseconomy.org/about/publications/report-2016 (accessed June 2018)

*New Plastics Economy Global Commitment*, June 2019. https://www.ellenmacarthurfoundation.org/news/spring-2019-report (accessed July 2019)

*Complete the Picture, How the Circular Economy Tackles Climate Change*, Sept 2019 report, www.ellenmacarthurfoundation.org/publications/completing-the-picture-climate-change (accessed Oct 2019)

European Bioplastics, "Environmental benefits of bioplastics," https://www.european-bioplastics.org/bioplastics/environment/ (accessed Nov 2019)

European Commission. *A European Strategy for Plastics in a Circular Economy*. 2018. https://ec.europa.eu/environment/circular-economy/pdf/plastics-strategy-brochure.pdf (accessed April 2019)

Fink, Larry. "A Sense of Purpose." *Larry Fink's Annual Letter to CEOs*, Nov 2018. www.blackrock.com/hk/en/insights/larry-fink-ceo-letter (accessed Feb 2019)

Gendall, Adam. "Design for Recycled Content Guide Launch." Presentation and Panel discussion at Sustainable Packaging Coalition Impact 2019 Conference, Seattle, Washington, April 1-4, 2019.

Grace, Robert. "In the Crosshairs: Single-Use, Disposable Packaging." *Plastics Engineering*, April 2019.

Green Tumble, "The Ecological Importance of Forest Fires", April 2016, https://greentumble.com/the-ecological-importance-of-forest-fires/ (accessed November 2019)

Griff, Alan. "Trying to understand 'plastiphobia'." *Plastics News,* July 1, 2019. https://www.plasticsnews.com/mailbag/trying-understand-plastiphobia (accessed Aug 2019)

Gore, Al. "An Inconvenient Truth." Pennsylvania: Rodale, 2006.

Goodrich, Nina. "Finding the balance: Re-assessing the use of materials." Presentation at Sustainable Packaging Coalition Impact 2019 Conference, Seattle, Washington, April 1-4, 2019.

Gray, Alex. "90% of plastic polluting our oceans comes from just 10 rivers." *World Economic Forum.* June 8, 2018. https://www.weforum.org/agenda/2018/06/90-of-plastic-polluting-our-oceans-comes-from-just-10-rivers/ (accessed August 2019)

GreenBiz. "Measuring Circularity: Why Life Cycle Assessment is Not the Right Tool." Webcast. Oct 23, 2018. https://www.greenbiz.com/webcast/measuring-circularity-why-life-cycle-assessment-not-right-tool (accessed April 2019)

Gutter, Rachel. "Creating Conditions for Agility for People, Products, and Platform." Presentation at Harvard University Executive Education for Sustainability Leadership, Cambridge, MA, Nov 5-9, 2018.

Hall, Ashley. "Walmart's Race to Recyclability." Presentation. Presentation at Sustainable Packaging Coalition Impact 2019 Conference, Seattle, Washington, April 1-4, 2019.

Hawken, Paul. *Drawdown.* New York: Penguin, 2017.

Haustrup, Camilla. "The Danish Forum for Circular Plastic Packaging." Presentation at EuPC conference Plastic Packaging and the EU Plastics Strategy, Brussels, Belgium, Sept 25, 2018.

Heim, Lawrence. *Killing Sustainability*, Self-pub., Amazon, 2018.

Hower, Mike. "Timberland retreads old tires as new shoes." *GreenBiz,* Nov 3, 2014. https://www.greenbiz.com/article/timberland-giving-old-tires-new-treads-new-shoes (accessed

Sept 2018)

Hsueh, Joe. "Systems Mapping for Systems Change." Presentation at Harvard University Executive Education for Sustainability Leadership, Cambridge, MA, Nov 5-9, 2018.

International Institute for Sustainable Development, "Sustainable Development", https://www.iisd.org/topic/sustainable-development (accessed Oct 2019)

Jagtop, Prashant. "A view of the future of sustainable packaging." Presentation at Sustainable Packaging Coalition Impact 2019 Conference, Seattle, Washington, April 1-4, 2019.

Johnson, Jim. "Defining recyclable on both sides of the Atlantic." *Plastics News,* July 2018.

"Berry takes multifaceted approach to sustainability." *Plastics News,* April 2019.

Kazakova, Tatjana. "When Purpose Drives Business Development." Presentation at Harvard University Executive Education for Sustainability Leadership, Cambridge, MA, Nov 5-9, 2018.

Laird, Karen. "Breaking down bioplastics." *Plastics News,* Feb 4, 2019.

Lazaridis, Nick. "In 2019, businesses will need to embrace sustainability, or risk being left behind." *edie.net,* Feb 2019. https://www.edie.net/blog/In-2019-businesses-will-need-to-embrace-sustainability-or-risk-being-left-behind/6098605 (accessed May 2019)

Leibson, Hayley. "The Power of Purpose Driven." *Forbes,* Jan 25, 2018. https://www.forbes.com/sites/hayleyleibson/2018/01/25/the-power-of-purpose-driven/#6c12b6f35dca (accessed March 2019)

Loepp, Don. "Plastics education stories are instructive and inspiring." *Plastics News,* July 2019.

Longo, Eugenio. "Borealis Circular Economy Solutions." Presentation at EuPC conference Plastic Packaging and the EU Plastics Strategy, Brussels, Belgium, Sept 25, 2018.

Materials Recovery For the Future, "Home", https://www. materialsrecoveryforthefuture.com/ (accessed 10/21/19)

McDonough, William & Braungart, Michael. *The Upcycle*. New York: North Point Press. 2013 & *Cradle to Cradle*. New York: North Point Press. 2002.

McGuire, Ken. "Peering into a crystal ball: Sustainable Packaging....in the Future!" Presentation. Presentation at Sustainable Packaging Coalition Impact 2019 Conference, Seattle, Washington, April 1-4, 2019.

Ministry of Environment and Food of Denmark Environmental Protection Agency. "Life Cycle Assessment of grocery carrier bags." Feb 2018. https://www2.mst.dk/udgiv/ publications/2018/02/978-87-93614-73-4.pdf (accessed July 2019)

Muth, Jon J. *Zen Shorts*. Singapore: Caldecott Honor. 2005.

Narayan, Ramani. "Bioplastics: Essential instruments in your sustainability orchestra." Presentation at Sustainable Packaging Coalition Impact 2019 Conference, Seattle, Washington, April 1-4, 2019.

National Park Service, "Yosemite," Nps.gov, https://www.nps. gov/yose/index.htm (accessed August 2019)

Northeast Recycling Council. *MRF Pilot & Flexible Packaging*. Webinar, Nov 2018.

Ocean Conservancy, "The Problem with Plastics," https:// oceanconservancy.org/trash-free-seas/plastics-in-the-ocean/ (accessed July 2019)

Osborne, Charlie. "In Amsterdam, there are more bicycled than people." *ZDNET* June 2013. https://www.zdnet.com/ article/in-amsterdam-there-are-more-bicycles-than-people/ (accessed Nov 2018)

Pack Expo International, "Overview," www.packexpointerna-tional.com/overview (accessed July 2019)

Parker, Laura. "We made it. We depend on it. We're drowning in it. Plastic." *National Geographic Magazine,* June 2018.

"The world's plastic pollution crisis explained", *National Geographic*, June 7, 2019, https://www.nationalgeographic.com/environment/habitats/plastic-pollution/#close (accessed Oct 2019)

Polymer Comply Europe. *The Usage of Recycled Plastics Materials by Plastics Converters in Europe*, 2017, https://design4recycling.org/uploads/1/1/7/9/117994545/eupc_survey-use-recycled-plastics_2017_pce-report.pdf (accessed Aug 2018)

Posacka, Anna. "Masterclass: What do we know about source and pathways of land-based microplastics?" Presentation at Sustainable Packaging Coalition Impact 2019 Conference, Seattle, Washington, April 1-4, 2019.

Potenza, Alessandra. "Are cotton totes better for the Earth than plastic bags? It depends on what you care about." *The Verge* May 2018. https://www.theverge.com/2018/5/12/17337602/plastic-tote-bags-climate-change-litter-life-cycle-assessments-environment (accessed July 2018).

Preston, Malcom. "Business as Usual." Presentation at Harvard University Executive Education for Sustainability Leadership, Cambridge, MA, Nov 5-9, 2018.

Project STOP, "About," www.stopoceanplastics.com/about/ (accessed Feb 2019)

Raworth, Kate. *Doughnut Economic*. Vermont: Chelsea Green Publishing, 2017.

Reiley, Laura. "They finally built a better ketchup bottle. And soon it's going to be everywhere." *Washington Post*. July 2018. https://www.washingtonpost.com/business/2019/07/09/they-finally-built-better-ketchup-bottle-soon-its-going-be-everywhere/ (accessed Aug 2019)

Roosegaarde, Dann. "Landscapes of the Future." Presentation at Sustainable Packaging Coalition Impact 2019 Conference, Seattle, Washington, April 1-4, 2019.

Ryan, David L. "Time to fully embrace composting, an idea that doesn't stink." *Boston Globe*, Oct 2018. https://www.

bostonglobe.com/opinion/editorials/2018/10/08/time-fully-embrace-composting-really/LCcdV0wfJRgcPS2kq9TRUL/story.html (accessed July 2019)

Sinek, Simon. *Start with Why*, New York: Penguin. 2009.

Schmidt, Isabell. "Eco Design of Plastic Packaging: The Round Table's Management Guidelines." Presentation at EuPC conference Plastic Packaging and the EU Plastics Strategy, Brussels, Belgium, Sept 25, 2018.

Sharp, Leith. "The Agility Imperative." Presentation at Harvard University Executive Education for Sustainability Leadership, Cambridge, MA, Nov 5-9, 2018.

"Sustainability Leadership: A North Star for the 21st Century." Presentation at Harvard University Executive Education for Sustainability Leadership, Cambridge, MA, Nov 5-9, 2018.

"Sustainability Leadership: Flow State Structures." Presentation at Harvard University Executive Education for Sustainability Leadership, Cambridge, MA, Nov 5-9, 2018.

Smith, Mark Evan. "Tenaya Lodge evacuated as Railroad Fire roars through Fish Camp", *Sierra Star,* August 29, 2017, https://www.sierrastar.com/news/local/article170067757.html (accessed November 2019)

Smith, Wayne. "Business Intelligence for Project Management: DIKUW (part 1)." Vertex Innovations Blog. https://www.vertex-us.com/blog/business-intelligence-for-project-management-dikuw-part-1 (accessed Aug 2019).

Starbucks' Stories and News, "Starbucks Roastery Earns LEED Platinum Certification," November 2015, https://stories.starbucks.com/stories/2015/starbucks-platinum-certification-for-roastery-and-2016-goals/ (accessed October 2019)

Sustainable Development Goals Knowledge Platform, "SDGS", https://sustainabledevelopment.un.org/sdgs (accessed August 2019)

Switzer, Nelson. "Plastic: From Linear to Circular" Presentation. Presentation at Sustainable Packaging Coalition Impact 2019

Conference, Seattle, Washington, April 1-4, 2019.

SPI—The Plastics Industry Trade Association. *Sustainability Benchmarking Survey*, 2015. https://www.plasticsindustry.org/ sites/default/files/2015BenchmarkingSurvey.pdf (accessed Jan 2019)

Szaky, Tom. *The Future of Packaging*, California: Berrett-Koehler Publishers. 2019.

Tan, Ashley. "From plogging to veganism: Is sustainability the new normal for consumers?" *Eco-Business*, Oct 2018. https:// www.eco-business.com/news/from-plogging-to-veganism-is-sustainability-the-new-normal-for-consumers/ (accessed July 2019)

Tipa Corp, "Products," https://tipa-corp.com/about-2/overview/ (accessed May 2019)

Tipaldo, Emily. "MRFF: Innovation, recycling and flexible plastic packaging." *Recycling Today.* May 2018. https://www. recyclingtoday.com/article/mrff-flexible-plastic-packaging-recycling/ (accessed June 2019)

Townsend, Solitaire. "88% of Consumers Want You To Help Them Make A Difference," *Forbes* Nov 21, 2018, https://www. forbes.com/sites/solitairetownsend/2018/11/21/consumers-want-you-to-help-them-make-a-difference/#672cac826954 (accessed Dec 2019)

Trim, Heather & others on panel. "Bans: Do they help transition from a linear to a circular economy?" Presentation at Sustainable Packaging Coalition Impact 2019 Conference, Seattle, Washington, April 1-4, 2019.

Toensmeier, Pat. "Almost Like New." *Plastic Engineering Magazine*, June 2019.

United Nations Environment Programme. *Single-Use Plastics: A Roadmap for Sustainability.* 2018. https://www.unenvironment. org/resources/report/single-use-plastics-roadmap-sustainability (accessed Jan 2019)

*UN Environment 2018 Annual Report*, 2018, www.unenvironment.

org/resources/un-environment-2018-annual-report    (access
June 2019)

*Exploring the potential for adopting alternative materials to reduce marine plastic litter.* 2018. https://www.unenvironment.org/resources/report/exploring-potential-adopting-alternative-materials-reduce-marine-plastic-litter (accessed Feb 2019)

*Our Planet is Drowning in Plastic Pollution,* 2018, https://www.unenvironment.org/interactive/beat-plastic-pollution/ (accessed Dec 2019)

United State Environmental Protection Agency, "Facts and Figures about Materials, Waste and Recycling," https://www.epa.gov/facts-and-figures-about-materials-waste-and-recycling/national-overview-facts-and-figures-materials (accessed October 2019)

US Small Business Administration Office of Advocacy, "2018 Small Business Profile," 2018, https://www.sba.gov/sites/default/files/advocacy/2018-Small-Business-Profiles-US.pdf (accessed Dec 2019)

Weber, Jerry. "Increasing Agility by Leading Adaptive and Hierarchical Network Strategy." Presentation at Harvard University Executive Education for Sustainability Leadership, Cambridge, MA, Nov 5-9, 2018.

Weigard, Julia. "The 30 Most Famous Harvard Students Of All Time," Business Insider May 3, 2010, https://www.businessinsider.com/30-most-famous-harvard-students-of-all-time-2010-4 (accessed September 2019)

Weston, Phoebe. "Plastic Bags were created to save the planet, inventor's son says," *Independent,* Oct 17, 2019, https://www.independent.co.uk/environment/plastic-bags-pollution-paper-cotton-tote-bags-environment-a9159731.html (accessed Jan 2020)

Wrap, "UK Plastic Pact," www.wrap.org.uk/content/the-uk-plastics-pact (accessed Jan 2019)

BUSINESS
BOOKS

# Business Books

Business Books publishes practical guides
and insightful non-fiction for beginners and professionals.
Covering aspects from management skills, leadership and
organizational change to positive work environments, career
coaching and self-care for managers, our books are a valuable
addition to those working in the world of business.

### 15 Ways to Own Your Future
Take Control of Your Destiny in Business and in Life
Michael Khouri
A 15-point blueprint for creating better collaboration, enjoyment,
and success in business and in life.
Paperback: 978-1-78535-300-0 ebook: 978-1-78535-301-7

### The Common Excuses of the Comfortable Compromiser
Understanding Why People Oppose Your Great Idea
Matt Crossman
Comfortable compromisers block the way of anyone trying to
change anything. This is your guide to their common excuses.
Paperback: 978-1-78099-595-3 ebook: 978-1-78099-596-0

## The Failing Logic of Money
Duane Mullin

Money is wasteful and cruel, causes war, crime and dysfunctional feudalism. Humankind needs happiness, peace and abundance. So banish money and use technology and knowledge to rid the world of war, crime and poverty.

Paperback: 978-1-84694-259-4 ebook: 978-1-84694-888-6

## Mastering the Mommy Track
Juggling Career and Kids in Uncertain Times
Erin Flynn Jay

*Mastering the Mommy Track* tells the stories of everyday working mothers, the challenges they have faced, and lessons learned.

Paperback: 978-1-78099-123-8 ebook: 978-1-78099-124-5

## Modern Day Selling
Unlocking Your Hidden Potential
Brian Barfield

Learn how to reconnect sales associates with customers and unlock hidden sales potential.

Paperback: 978-1-78099-457-4 ebook: 978-1-78099-458-1

## The Most Creative, Escape the Ordinary, Excel at Public Speaking Book Ever
All The Help You Will Ever Need in Giving a Speech
Philip Theibert

The 'everything you need to give an outstanding speech' book, complete with original material written by a professional speech-writer.

Paperback: 978-1-78099-672-1 ebook: 978-1-78099-673-8

## On Business And For Pleasure
A Self-Study Workbook for Advanced Business English
Michael Berman
This workbook includes enjoyable challenges and has been designed to help students with the English they need for work.
Paperback: 978-1-84694-304-1


## Small Change, Big Deal
Money as if People Mattered
Jennifer Kavanagh
Money is about relationships: between individuals and between communities. Small is still beautiful, as peer lending model, micro-credit, shows.
Paperback: 978-1-78099-313-3 ebook: 978-1-78099-314-0